VEGETABLE

GARDENERS BIBLE

The Ultimate Guide to a Lush, Organic Bounty: Master Year-Round Harvests, Foolproof Pest Control, and Secret Soil Techniques—Even If You've Never Planted a Seed

Leroy Karper

TABLE OF CONTENTS

Herbal Infusions and Benefits 174

Celebrating Your Bounty: Hosting a Garden-to-Table

Dinner 185

BOOK 1: THE FOUNDATIONS OF VEGETABLE GARDENING

Embarking on the journey of vegetable gardening is akin to beginning a profound dialogue with the earth—a dialogue that teaches us about the cycles of life, the importance of patience, and the rewards of mindful stewardship. As we delve into **The Foundations of Vegetable Gardening**, we are not just learning to cultivate plants; we are learning to cultivate life, resilience, and community. This chapter is designed to lay the groundwork for a gardening practice that is as nurturing to the gardener as it is to the earth it seeks to tend.

At the heart of this journey is the understanding that gardening is much more than a hobby or a means to produce fresh, organic produce. It is a transformative process that connects us deeply to the natural world, offering lessons in ecology, sustainability, and the interconnectedness of all life. Through the act of gardening, we participate in a cycle that has sustained humanity for millennia, and in doing so, we link our efforts to those of gardener's past, present, and future.

Soil: The Lifeblood of the Garden

Our exploration begins with the soil—the lifeblood of the garden. Understanding soil is not merely about knowing its types or how to amend it; it's about recognizing soil as a living, breathing entity that nurtures and sustains. We'll dive into the importance of building healthy soil, the bedrock upon which all successful gardens are built.

Water and Light: The Essentials of Life

Just as crucial are the elements of water and light—each plant's source of life and energy. Mastering the art of watering and learning to work with the natural light your garden receives are pivotal skills. These sections aim to deepen your understanding of these fundamental requirements, guiding you in creating a garden that thrives.

Planting with Purpose

Planting is not just the act of placing seeds in the ground; it's a thoughtful process of selection, timing, and placement. We'll explore how to choose the right plants for your garden's specific conditions and how to time your plantings to take advantage of natural cycles and seasons.

The Journey Ahead

As we move through this chapter, we invite you to view each step as part of a larger journey—a journey not just toward harvests of vegetables, but toward a deeper understanding of and connection with the natural world. Gardening is a practice of observation, experimentation, and adaptation. It is a path that can lead to not only a bountiful garden but also a more sustainable way of living.

The Foundations of Vegetable Gardening is your gateway to a world where the act of gardening is an act of love—love for the earth, love for life, and love for the future. Let's embark on this journey together, with open hearts and willing hands, ready to nurture and be nurtured by the gardens we grow.

INTRODUCTION TO ORGANIC GARDENING

Embarking on the path of organic gardening is akin to opening a door to a world where each plant tells a story, and every handful of soil holds the promise of life. It's not merely a method of gardening; it's a philosophy that intertwines the health of our bodies with the wellbeing of the earth. This journey is about embracing the cycle of life in its most natural form, nurturing plants without the aid of synthetic chemicals, and in return, reaping vegetables that are not only a feast for the eyes but a bounty for the health.

The Essence of Organic Gardening

At its core, organic gardening is the practice of growing vegetables, fruits, and flowers using only substances derived from living things and avoiding synthetic fertilizers and pesticides. This approach focuses on building a healthy ecosystem where plants thrive naturally. It's about working *with* nature, rather than against it. The essence lies in understanding that everything in your garden is connected—from the tiniest microorganism in the soil to the tallest sunflower reaching for the sky.

Soil: The Foundation of Your Garden

The heart of organic gardening beats beneath the surface, in the rich, dark soil that cradles the roots of your plants. Healthy soil teeming with life is the cornerstone of any successful garden. This soil is a living, breathing entity, home to a complex web of organisms that work in harmony to break down organic matter, aerate the earth, and make nutrients available to your plants. Feeding your soil with compost, manure, and other organic matter enriches it, building the foundation for a thriving garden.

Choosing Organic Seeds

Embarking on your gardening journey begins with selecting the right seeds. Opting for organic seeds is a commitment to preserving biodiversity and supporting practices that are in harmony with the environment. These seeds come from plants that have been grown organically, ensuring that they are well-adapted to thriving without chemical aids. By choosing organic, you're not just planting a garden; you're sowing the seeds of an ecological legacy.

Natural Pest and Disease Management

One of the most compelling chapters in the organic gardening story revolves around managing pests and diseases without resorting to synthetic chemicals. This narrative is not about eliminating every insect or blotch on a leaf but about creating a balanced ecosystem where natural predators and plant health keep potential problems in check. Introducing beneficial insects, practicing crop rotation, and selecting disease-resistant varieties are chapters in this tale of ecological harmony.

Companion Planting: Nature's Harmony

Companion planting is akin to composing a symphony, where each plant plays a role that supports and enhances the others. This practice is based on the understanding that certain plants, when grown together, can improve each other's health and yields. For example, marigolds emit a scent that repels harmful pests, while beans fix nitrogen in the soil, enriching it for neighboring plants. It's about creating plant communities where each member brings something valuable to the table.

Water Wisdom: Conserving Life's Essence

Water is the lifeblood of your garden, and in organic gardening, how you water is as important as how often. Utilizing rainwater, practicing drip irrigation, and mulching to retain soil moisture are all strokes in the art of sustainable water use. It's about giving your plants the hydration they need while respecting the precious nature of water as a resource.

Organic gardening is a dance to the rhythm of nature's seasons. Each season plays its part in the lifecycle of your garden, from the quiet dormancy of winter to the explosive growth of summer. Understanding these rhythms—and the unique opportunities and challenges they present—is key to a garden that flourishes year-round. This knowledge guides your actions, from planting to harvest, ensuring that your garden works in harmony with the natural world.

Harvesting: The Fruits of Your Labor

The climax of the organic gardening journey is the harvest—when you get to reap what you've sown. This moment is about more than just picking vegetables; it's a celebration of the success of your organic practices. Harvesting at the right time and in the right way ensures that your garden continues to produce and that you enjoy the freshest, most flavorful produce possible.

The Community of Gardeners

Organic gardening is not a solitary endeavor; it's a chapter in the larger story of a community of gardeners. Sharing seeds, experiences, and harvests connects you to a network of like-minded individuals who are all contributing to a more sustainable, healthy world. This community is a source of support, inspiration, and friendship, making the gardening journey all the more rewarding.

Embracing the Organic Lifestyle

Adopting organic gardening practices is the first step in a broader commitment to living a sustainable, eco-friendly lifestyle. It's a choice that impacts not just your garden, but also the world around you. By choosing organic, you're voting for a future where the environment is respected, where food is pure and wholesome, and where the connection between the earth and its inhabitants is honored.

As you turn the pages of this subchapter and embark on your organic gardening adventure, remember that each plant you grow, every insect you observe, and every handful of soil you nurture is a testament to the power of working in harmony with nature. Organic gardening is more than a method—it's a movement towards a healthier world, one garden at a time.

CHOOSING THE RIGHT LOCATION

In the grand tapestry of gardening, choosing the right location for your vegetable garden is akin to setting the stage for a play. The success of the actors—your plants—relies heavily on this initial backdrop. It's a decision that shapes the journey of your garden from a mere plot of land to a thriving haven of bounty. This choice is not

merely about finding a spot; it's about creating a harmony between the elements and your garden, ensuring that every plant can perform to its full potential.

Sunlight: The Lifeblood of Your Garden

At the heart of this stage-setting is sunlight—the lifeblood of your garden. Vegetables are sun worshippers, craving at least six to eight hours of direct sunlight each day. The right location basks in this golden glow, ensuring that your plants receive the energy they need to photosynthesize, grow, and produce. Observing potential spots throughout the day helps you understand the sun's path and identify the ideal location that captures its rays.

Water Access: A Critical Element

Water, the essence of life, plays a crucial role in selecting your garden's location. Proximity to a water source simplifies the task of keeping your garden hydrated. Whether it's a nearby hose, a rain barrel, or an automated irrigation system, easy water access ensures that your plants never thirst unnecessarily. In the grand scheme, a garden near water is a garden that's half nurtured already.

Soil Quality: The Foundation of Growth

The quality of the soil in your chosen location is the foundation upon which your garden grows. Rich, fertile, well-draining soil is the ideal stage for your vegetable actors to thrive. Before committing to a spot, get to know its soil. Is it sandy, loamy, or clay-heavy? The answer shapes your gardening strategies, from amending the soil to choosing plants suited to its texture. Sometimes, the best location is made, not found, through the addition of organic matter and compost to enrich and improve the soil's structure.

Wind and Exposure: The Unseen Forces

Wind and exposure to the elements can play friend or foe to your garden. A location sheltered from harsh winds and protected from winter's cold grasp is a sanctuary for your plants. Consider natural windbreaks like fences, hedges, or the walls of your home to shield your garden. However, beware of creating a microclimate that's too sheltered, which can inhibit airflow and encourage disease.

Space and Expansion: Thinking Ahead

As you select the location for your garden, think not just of the present but also of the future. A garden is a living, growing entity with aspirations of its own. Allow room for expansion as your gardening skills flourish and your ambitions grow. A spot that accommodates raised beds, containers, and possibly even a small greenhouse or garden shed is a location that sees not just the garden of today but the garden of tomorrow.

Visibility and Accessibility: The Heart's Connection

A garden that's out of sight often becomes out of mind. Choose a location that you'll see regularly, ensuring that your garden remains a central part of your daily life. This visibility fosters a deep connection, reminding you to tend to its needs and revel in its successes. Accessibility is equally important. A garden that's easy to reach and navigate invites more care and interaction, turning gardening tasks from chores into cherished routines.

Compatibility with Lifestyle and Aesthetics

Your garden should be a reflection of your lifestyle and aesthetics. A location that integrates seamlessly into your outdoor living space not only enhances the beauty of your surroundings but also invites you to spend more time among your plants. Consider how your garden complements your home and lifestyle. Whether it's a culinary garden just steps from your kitchen or a decorative plot that enhances your outdoor entertaining area, the right location marries functionality with beauty.

Observation and Intuition: The Gardener's Tools

Choosing the right location is as much about observation as it is about intuition. Spend time in your potential garden spot at different times of the day and year. Notice how the elements interact with the space. Feel the energy of the place. Sometimes, the best location for your garden is where your instinct tells you it belongs.

Embracing Challenges and Making Adjustments

Even the most carefully chosen location may present challenges. Shade from a growing tree, soil that's less than ideal, or unexpected water runoff can all impact your garden. Embrace these challenges as opportunities to learn and grow as a gardener. Making adjustments, whether it's pruning a tree to allow more sunlight or improving drainage, is part of the gardening journey.

The Joy of the First Step

Selecting the location for your garden is the first step in a journey that's as rewarding as it is enriching. It's a choice that sets the tone for your gardening adventure, a decision that weaves together the elements, your ambitions, and the inherent beauty of growing your own food. In this spot, you'll not just grow vegetables; you'll cultivate memories, experiences, and a deeper connection to the earth.

As you stand in the chosen location for your garden, imagine the future it holds. See in your mind's eye the shoots breaking through the soil, the plants reaching towards the sun, and the harvest that awaits. This is where it all begins. With the right location, your garden is already on its way to becoming a thriving, vibrant testament to the beauty and bounty of nature.

UNDERSTANDING YOUR CLIMATE AND SEASONS

Understanding your climate and the rhythmic dance of the seasons is akin to learning the language of your garden. This knowledge is not merely academic; it's the heartbeat of successful gardening. Just as a musician must know their instrument, a gardener must know the climate and seasons to play the symphony of growth successfully.

The Tapestry of Climate Zones

The planet's vast and varied climate zones are like distinct neighborhoods, each with its own weather patterns, seasonal changes, and unique gardening challenges and opportunities. From the frost-bound silence of the north to the sun-drenched warmth of the tropics, knowing where your garden lies on this tapestry is crucial. This knowledge isn't just about what you can grow, but also how and when to grow it. The USDA Hardiness Zone Map and the Sunset Climate Zones provide invaluable guidance, offering a baseline for understanding the plants best suited to your garden's locale.

Seasonal Rhythms and Their Significance

The year's cycle into spring, summer, autumn, and winter isn't just a backdrop for your garden; it's a guide for your gardening activities. Each season plays its part in the life of your garden:

- **Spring** whispers promises of renewal, a time to prepare the soil, start seeds, and plant early crops under the watchful eye of the last frosts.
- **Summer** is the full-throated song of growth, warmth, and abundance, where the garden reaches its peak, demanding attention to watering, weeding, and warding off pests.
- **Autumn** brings a time of harvest and reflection, as well as preparation for the colder months. It's a season for planting cool-weather crops and beginning the cycle of soil enrichment for the next year.
- **Winter** offers a pause, a quiet moment for the garden and gardener to rest. It's a time for planning, for dreaming of the next cycle of growth, and for taking care of the infrastructure that supports your garden.

Microclimates: The Garden's Microcosm

Even within your garden, there exist microclimates—small pockets where conditions differ from the general climate. These can be created by buildings, fences, bodies of water, or even the garden's own layout. Understanding these microenvironments allows you to fine-tune your garden, placing plants in the optimal conditions for their growth. A shady spot might nurture a lush herb garden, while a sun-trapped wall could be the perfect backdrop for heat-loving tomatoes.

Adapting to Your Climate

Adapting to your climate means more than just surviving; it's about thriving. It involves selecting plant varieties that are suited to your region's peculiarities, from drought-resistant species in arid zones to cold-hardy varieties in cooler climates. It's also about timing—knowing when to sow seeds and when to harvest, tailored to the unique cadence of your local seasons.

Water: A Precious Resource

In every climate, water plays a pivotal role. Whether you're blessed with abundant rainfall or navigating the challenges of drought, how you manage water in your garden is a reflection of your understanding of the climate. Techniques such as rainwater harvesting, drip irrigation, and mulching are not just water-saving measures; they're acts of stewardship, of aligning your garden practices with the rhythms of nature.

The Changing Climate and Your Garden

As the world's climate evolves, so too must our gardening practices. An understanding of your local climate today must be tempered with an awareness of how it might change tomorrow. This may mean adjusting planting dates, diversifying plant selections, or implementing new water management strategies. The resilient gardener is one who observes, learns, and adapts to these changes, ensuring their garden remains a vibrant and productive oasis in a changing world.

Celebrating the Seasons

More than just a framework for gardening activities, the seasons offer a rhythm to life in the garden that connects us to the natural world. Celebrating these changes, from the first spring blossom to the last autumn leaf, enriches our gardening experience. It reminds us that our gardens are not just spaces of cultivation but places of connection—to the earth, to the cycles of life, and to ourselves.

In Harmony with Nature

Ultimately, understanding your climate and seasons is about seeking harmony with nature. It's a journey of discovery, learning how to listen to the whispers of the wind, the teachings of the rain, and the wisdom of the earth. This harmony leads to a garden that is not just a place of growth but a sanctuary of peace, a testament to the beauty and abundance that comes when we garden in tune with the world around us.

In this dance with the seasons, you become more than just a gardener; you become a caretaker of a small piece of the earth, a steward of its cycles and seasons. Your garden becomes a living canvas, painted with the colors of the harvest, animated by the rhythms of the climate, and enriched by the understanding and respect you bring to your role in its care.

ESSENTIAL TOOLS AND EQUIPMENT

In the orchestra of gardening, your tools and equipment are the instruments that bring the symphony to life. These essentials, ranging from the humble trowel to the sturdy wheelbarrow, are not just accessories but extensions of the gardener's hand, each playing a crucial role in cultivating a thriving vegetable garden. This chapter is dedicated to unveiling the essential tools and equipment that every gardener should have in their repertoire, ensuring that your gardening journey is as smooth and enjoyable as possible.

The Spade and Shovel: Your Gardening Allies

At the very heart of gardening tools lie the spade and shovel. These are your allies in turning the soil, planting, and moving earth. A good spade with a sharp edge is indispensable for slicing through sod and digging planting holes, while a shovel, with its scooping shape, is perfect for moving soil and compost. Choose tools with a comfortable handle and a sturdy blade that can withstand the rigors of garden work.

The Rake: More Than Meets the Eye

A rake might seem simple, but it's a multi-faceted tool essential for smoothing soil, clearing debris, and preparing seedbeds. A garden rake with metal tines is perfect for breaking up clumps of soil and creating a fine tilth for sowing seeds. Meanwhile, a leaf rake, with its wider and more flexible tines, is indispensable for clearing leaves and other garden debris.

Hoes: The Versatile Weeders

The hoe is your primary weapon in the ongoing battle against weeds. With various types available, from the traditional draw hoe for chopping weeds to the stirrup hoe for a gentler slicing action, choosing the right hoe can make weeding less of a chore. Hoes are also useful for creating furrows for planting seeds and aerating the soil around plants.

Trowels and Hand Forks: The Garden's Precision Tools

For up-close work, such as planting seedlings, transplanting flowers, and weeding, a good hand trowel and fork are indispensable. These tools allow for precision work in tight spaces, ensuring that your plants are handled with care. Look for ergonomically designed handles to reduce strain on your hands during prolonged use.

Secateurs: The Pruner's Companion

A sharp pair of secateurs (or pruning shears) is crucial for cutting back plants, pruning fruit bushes, and deadheading flowers. Opt for a pair that fits comfortably in your hand and can be easily disassembled for cleaning and sharpening. Bypass secateurs, with their scissor-like action, are preferable for making clean cuts on living plants.

Watering Can and Hose: The Life Givers

Water is the essence of life in your garden, and having the right tools for watering is essential. A watering can with a detachable rose allows for gentle watering of seedlings and young plants, preventing soil displacement. For larger gardens, a hose with an adjustable nozzle or a sprinkler system can save time and ensure even watering.

Wheelbarrow: The Heavy Lifter

A sturdy wheelbarrow is indispensable for moving heavy loads around the garden, from soil and compost to garden waste and harvested vegetables. Choose a wheelbarrow that is lightweight yet durable, with a comfortable grip and an easy-to-manage wheel configuration for navigating garden paths.

Garden Gloves: Protecting Your Hands

Gardening is a hands-on activity, and a good pair of gloves is essential to protect your hands from thorns, splinters, and soil-borne pathogens. Gloves also provide a better grip on tools. Select gloves that are durable, provide dexterity, and fit your hands well.

Garden Fork: The Soil Aerator

A garden fork is an invaluable tool for turning soil, aerating compacted earth, and breaking up hard ground. Its tines can reach deep into the soil, making it easier to incorporate compost and other organic matter. A fork is also handy for lifting and dividing perennials.

Gardening Knife: The Handy Cutter

A gardening knife, or Hori Hori, is a versatile tool for cutting, digging, and even measuring planting depth. Its serrated edge is ideal for slicing through roots or cutting open bags of compost, while the pointed end can be used for planting bulbs or weeding.

Tool Maintenance: Keeping Your Instruments in Tune

Just as a musician cares for their instruments, a gardener must maintain their tools to ensure they remain in good working order. Regular cleaning, sharpening, and oiling of tools not only prolongs their life but also makes gardening tasks more efficient and enjoyable. A well-maintained tool is a joy to use and can become a trusted companion in your gardening adventures.

Embracing the Essentials

These tools and equipment are the foundational elements of your gardening practice, each serving a specific purpose that aids in the creation and maintenance of a vibrant garden. However, it's not just about having the right tools but also about using them effectively. As you grow in your gardening journey, you'll discover which tools work best for you, refining your selection to match your garden's unique needs.

Remember, the best garden is not necessarily the one with the most expensive or most extensive array of tools but the one tended with care, attention, and a deep love for the act of gardening itself. With these essential tools in hand, you're well-equipped to cultivate a space of growth, beauty, and tranquility, where the fruits of your labor are not just the vegetables on your table but the joy and satisfaction that comes from tending the earth.

CONCLUSION

As we draw the curtain on this exploration of *The Foundations of Vegetable Gardening*, it's important to pause and reflect on the journey we've undertaken together. From the first stirrings of interest in organic practices to the final touches of choosing the right tools and equipment, each step has been a stone laid on the path to creating a garden that is not just a source of sustenance but a haven of biodiversity, a sanctuary for the soul, and a testament to the gardener's connection with the earth.

Gardening, as we've discovered, is much more than the act of planting seeds and watching them grow. It's a dance with the natural world, a partnership that teaches us about patience, resilience, and the intricate web of life that sustains us all. The lessons learned in the garden—about the importance of nurturing the soil, understanding the climate and seasons, and selecting the right tools—are metaphors for life itself. They teach us that with careful preparation, a deep understanding of our environment, and the right resources, we can cultivate not only plants but our well-being.

In embarking on this gardening journey, we've embraced the philosophy that every garden, no matter its size, is a microcosm of the world at large. By choosing to garden organically, to work in harmony with nature rather than against it, we make a stand for sustainability and stewardship of our planet. We've learned that the garden is a place of endless learning, where every failure is a lesson and every success a celebration. It's a space where the cycles of life—from the decay of compost to the blooming of a flower—are on full display, reminding us of the beauty and fragility of existence.

The garden, with its challenges and triumphs, is also a mirror reflecting our relationship with the world. It teaches us about care, attention, and the impact of our actions. As gardeners, we become custodians of our little patch of earth, with the power to influence the health of the soil, the quality of the water, and the diversity of life it supports. This responsibility is a call to action, a reminder that in nurturing our garden, we contribute to the well-being of the earth itself.

As this chapter of our gardening journey closes, let us carry forward the knowledge and insights we've gained, not as an end but as a foundation upon which to build. Let the garden be a place of continual discovery, where curiosity leads to experimentation and experimentation to growth. Let it be a source of joy, where the simple acts of planting a seed or turning the soil can bring a sense of peace and connection to the rhythms of nature.

In the end, the true harvest of the garden is not just the vegetables we grow but the growth within ourselves. Gardening cultivates patience, nurtures mindfulness, and fosters an appreciation for the complex beauty of the natural world. It challenges us to live more sustainably, to think more holistically, and to act with more care for the world around us.

As we look to the future, let our gardens be a testament to our commitment to the earth, to our communities, and to ourselves. May they be spaces of abundance, where the seeds we sow grow into sources of nourishment, inspiration, and hope. And may the lessons learned within their bounds inspire us to cultivate not just our gardens but a better world for generations to come.

In closing, remember that the journey of gardening is one without end, a path that winds through seasons of change, growth, and renewal. As you continue on this path, keep your hands in the soil and your heart open to the lessons it teaches. For in the garden, as in life, there is always more to discover, more to cherish, and more to nurture. Happy gardening, and may your garden flourish in abundance and joy.

BOOK 2: SOIL MASTERY AND PREPARATION

In the intricate dance of gardening, where the ballet of blossoms and the symphony of sprouts play out under the sun's watchful eye, there lies a performer so crucial yet so often unsung: the soil. This chapter, dedicated to the mastery and preparation of soil, is more than just a collection of techniques and tips. It's a homage to the very foundation of gardening, a deep dive into understanding, nurturing, and co-creating with the earth beneath our feet. For in the heart of every gardener beats the desire not just to grow plants, but to cultivate a vibrant, thriving ecosystem that begins with rich, fertile soil.

Soil is the soul of the garden, the repository of life, history, and potential. It's where the alchemical magic of turning seed into sustenance happens, under the watchful eyes of billions of microorganisms, in the embrace of organic matter, and within the complex dance of minerals and elements. To embark on the journey of soil mastery is to commit oneself to a lifetime of learning, observing, and respecting the cycles of nature that play out in this dark, rich medium.

The Living Soil: A Universe Underfoot

Every handful of healthy soil is teeming with life, a complex ecosystem that mirrors the diversity and interdependence found in the world above. Understanding this living soil is the first step toward mastery, a step that involves recognizing the soil as a partner in the gardening process. It's a dynamic entity, one that breathes, consumes, and transforms, facilitating the cycle of life that sustains all terrestrial ecosystems. This chapter will guide you through the microscopic universe beneath our feet, introducing the bacteria, fungi, nematodes, and other organisms that are the true cultivators of our gardens.

The Alchemy of Composting: Turning Waste into Gold

Central to soil preparation is the practice of composting, the transformation of organic waste into a nutrient-rich amendment that feeds the soil and, by extension, our plants. Composting is an act of environmental stewardship, a way of returning to the earth what we take from it and closing the loop in our garden ecosystems. We'll explore the science and art of composting, from the basics of building a compost pile to advanced techniques for accelerating decomposition, ensuring that you can create black gold in your backyard.

Building Soil Structure: The Architecture of Fertility

Soil structure—the way in which sand, silt, clay, and organic matter aggregate—determines the soil's ability to hold water, exchange gases, and support plant roots. Building and maintaining this structure is akin to constructing the foundation for a building, requiring careful attention and ongoing maintenance. This section will teach you how to enhance soil structure through amendments, cultivation practices, and the judicious use of cover crops, creating an ideal environment for plant roots to explore.

Balancing the Soil's Chemistry: The Nutrient Network

Just as our bodies require a balanced diet to thrive, so too do plants need a well-rounded suite of nutrients available in the soil. The chemistry of the soil, from its pH to its concentrations of nitrogen, phosphorus, potassium, and trace minerals, can dramatically affect plant health and productivity. We'll delve into the methods for assessing soil fertility, adjusting imbalances, and ensuring that your garden has the full spectrum of nutrients needed for vibrant growth.

Water Wise: Managing Moisture for Maximum Vitality

Water is the lifeblood of the garden, and the soil's ability to manage moisture is critical to plant health. Too little water and plants wither; too much and roots suffocate. This

chapter will cover strategies for optimizing water use in the garden, from improving soil's water-holding capacity with organic matter to implementing efficient irrigation practices that conserve water and target plant roots directly.

A Tapestry of Plants: Designing with Soil in Mind

The ultimate expression of soil mastery is a garden that thrives, a diverse tapestry of plants that are suited to the soil's unique characteristics. Choosing the right plants for your soil type, understanding how different plants interact with the soil, and designing planting schemes that improve soil health over time are all part of this intricate dance. We'll explore how to select and arrange plants in a way that celebrates the soil's potential, creating a garden that is not only beautiful but also ecologically sound.

The Gardener's Journey: From Soil Steward to Ecosystem Guardian

In the end, mastering soil and its preparation is not just a matter of applying techniques and following recipes. It's a journey of transformation, one that requires us to become stewards of the land, attentive to the needs of the soil and the life it supports. This chapter is your guide on that journey, offering the knowledge and inspiration needed to turn the act of gardening into an act of ecological restoration.

As we embark on this exploration of soil mastery and preparation, remember that every garden is a reflection of the soil from which it springs. By becoming caretakers of this essential resource, we not only enrich our gardens but also contribute to the health of our planet. So let us proceed with reverence for the soil, mindful of its complexity, its vitality, and its central role in the garden's ecosystem. Together, we'll learn to nurture the soil, that it might nurture us in return, in the endless cycle of growth and renewal that defines the art of gardening.

THE SCIENCE OF SOIL HEALTH

Diving into the realm of soil health is akin to exploring a hidden world beneath our feet, a world teeming with life and complexity. Soil is not just dirt; it's a living, breathing entity, the foundation of all terrestrial life, including our precious vegetable gardens. Understanding the science of soil health is crucial for every gardener who dreams of lush, bountiful harvests.

The Life Within: Soil's Living Ecosystem

Soil health hinges on its biology—on the myriad of organisms, from bacteria and fungi to earthworms and insects, that call it home. These microscopic and macroscopic life forms form a complex ecosystem that transforms dead matter into rich humus, cycles nutrients, improves soil structure, and fights off pathogens. The healthier your soil, the more vibrant this ecosystem is, leading to a self-sustaining garden that requires fewer inputs over time.

Soil Structure and Texture: The Building Blocks

The feel of soil—its texture—is determined by the proportions of sand, silt, and clay it contains. This texture affects water retention, drainage, and the ease with which roots can penetrate the soil. Structure, on the other hand, refers to how these particles clump together, creating spaces for air and water—critical for root growth and microbial activity. A soil with good structure allows for the delicate balance of moisture and aeration that plants need to thrive.

The Role of Organic Matter: Soil's Superfood

Organic matter is the cornerstone of soil health, serving as both a nutrient reservoir and a binder that improves soil structure. It includes anything once living, from fallen leaves and decaying plants to compost and manure. As it decomposes, organic matter releases nutrients in a form that plants can absorb, fosters microbial life, and acts as a sponge, holding water in the soil where plants can access it.

Water and Air: The Breath and Blood of Soil

Healthy soil manages water efficiently, storing it for when plants need it and draining excess to prevent root rot. This delicate balance is achieved through soil structure and organic matter, which create pores for water and air. Air in the soil, especially oxygen, is just as vital, fueling root and microbial respiration. Without adequate aeration, plants can't take up nutrients effectively, stunting their growth.

pH: Soil's Sweet Spot

Soil pH—a measure of its acidity or alkalinity—significantly affects plant health by influencing nutrient availability. Most vegetables thrive in slightly acidic to neutral soil (pH 6.0 to 7.0), where essential nutrients like nitrogen, phosphorus, and potassium are most readily available. Testing your soil's pH and adjusting it gently with organic amendments can unlock its full fertility potential.

Nutrient Cycles: The Circulatory System of the Garden

Understanding the nutrient cycles within your soil is crucial to maintaining its health. Nutrients move from the soil to the plant and back again in a continuous loop, aided by microbial decomposers. Organic gardening practices, such as composting and mulching, feed this cycle, reducing the need for synthetic fertilizers and creating a garden that grows more resilient and productive with each season.

Building Soil Health: Practices for the Wise Gardener

Building and maintaining soil health is an ongoing journey, one that rewards patience and care. Incorporating organic matter regularly, practicing crop rotation, and growing cover crops are just a few strategies that enrich soil life. Minimizing soil disturbance preserves microbial networks and reduces erosion, while mulching conserves moisture, suppresses weeds, and feeds the soil as it breaks down.

The Human Touch: Stewards of the Soil

As gardeners, we are more than just caretakers of plants; we are stewards of the soil. Our practices can either deplete and degrade this vital resource or enrich and regenerate it for future generations. Choosing the latter path means embracing a holistic approach to gardening, where the health of the soil is seen as inseparable from the health of the plants, ourselves, and the planet.

In essence, the science of soil health teaches us that gardening is not just about what we grow but how we grow it. By understanding and nurturing the complex web of life beneath our feet, we unlock the full potential of our gardens and step into a deeper, more sustainable relationship with the earth. This journey into soil mastery is not just a path to better gardening but a commitment to a healthier world.

COMPOSTING: BLACK GOLD FOR YOUR GARDEN

In the heart of every flourishing vegetable garden lies a secret, almost magical ingredient, reminiscent of ancient alchemy yet grounded in the humblest of garden practices. This treasure, known colloquially as "black gold," is none other than compost. It's the lifeblood of any garden, a testament to nature's resilience and capacity for renewal. Composting is not merely a method of waste disposal but a fundamental principle of organic gardening, embodying the cycle of life, death, and rebirth that sustains our entire ecosystem.

At its core, composting is the process of transforming kitchen scraps, yard waste, and other organic matter into a rich, soil-like substance through natural decomposition. This substance is teeming with beneficial microorganisms, essential nutrients, and the kind of organic matter that plants crave. It's what turns a good garden into a great garden, enabling vegetables to thrive where they might otherwise languish.

The Alchemy of Composting

To understand composting, think of it as a culinary art where the ingredients must be carefully balanced to create the perfect dish. Your compost pile or bin is the kitchen, and the organic matter you add is like a recipe that will be cooked over time, transforming into a nutrient-rich humus.

The recipe for compost has four basic ingredients: browns (carbon-rich materials), greens (nitrogen-rich materials), water, and air. Browns are your dried leaves, straw, and branches, providing the carbon that feeds the microorganisms. Greens are your kitchen scraps, grass clippings, and coffee grounds, supplying the nitrogen that fuels the decomposition process. Water and air are the invisible ingredients, critical for maintaining the pile's moisture and oxygen levels, ensuring that the microorganisms thrive and break down the materials efficiently.

The Process: Turning Scraps into Soil

The magic of composting begins when you layer these ingredients in your compost bin or pile. Aim for a balanced mix of browns and greens to prevent odors and ensure a speedy decomposition. Too many greens, and your compost may become slimy and smelly. Too many browns, and the process slows down, stalling the transformation. Water your pile to keep it as moist as a wrung-out sponge, and turn it every few weeks to aerate it, which helps speed up the decomposition by providing oxygen to the microorganisms at work. Over time, these ingredients will break down, and your pile will shrink in size, a sign that your compost is nearing readiness.

The Benefits of Black Gold

The benefits of adding compost to your garden are manifold. Firstly, it improves soil structure, making it more friable and better at retaining moisture, which is particularly beneficial during dry spells. It also enhances the soil's ability to hold nutrients, making those nutrients more available to plants. This reduces the need for synthetic fertilizers, which can be harmful to the environment and your health.

Moreover, compost introduces beneficial microorganisms to the soil. These microorganisms can break down organic matter into nutrients that plants can absorb, suppress plant diseases, and even help combat pests. In essence, compost doesn't just feed plants; it builds a vibrant, living soil ecosystem.

Crafting Your Compost Pile

You don't need a large space or special equipment to start composting. A simple pile in a corner of your yard or a basic compost bin can suffice. There are many styles of compost bins available, from rotating tumblers to stationary bins, each with its advantages. The key is to start small and simple, learning as you go what works best for your garden's needs and your lifestyle.

Add your kitchen scraps (avoiding meat, dairy, and oils, which can attract pests and create odors), along with yard waste, ensuring a good mix of browns and greens. If you're in an urban setting without access to a lot of yard waste, shredded cardboard or newspaper can serve as a brown material.

Troubleshooting Common Composting Challenges

Composting is an organic process, and like any garden activity, it can come with its set of challenges. A well-maintained compost pile should not smell bad. If it does, it's usually a sign that the pile is too wet or has too many greens. Adding more browns and turning the pile to introduce air can quickly remedy this.

If the composting process seems slow, it might need more nitrogen. Add more green materials, or consider a compost activator to jumpstart the process. And if pests are a problem, ensure that food scraps are buried well within the pile, and consider a bin with a lid or wire mesh at the bottom to deter them.

The Reward: Black Gold for Your Garden

When your compost is dark, crumbly, and smells like earth, it's ready to use. Spread it in your garden beds, mix it with potting soil, or use it as a top dressing around plants. Watching your garden respond to compost is a gratifying experience. Vegetables grow more vigorously, flowers bloom more profusely, and the soil becomes a living tapestry teeming with life.

Composting closes the loop, turning what would be waste into a valuable resource. It's a concrete step toward sustainable living, reducing landfill waste and cutting down on greenhouse gas emissions from decomposing organic matter. Moreover, it's a deeply satisfying practice, connecting us more closely to the cycles of nature.

In the end, composting isn't just about producing better yields or healthier plants. It's a reflection of the gardener's commitment to stewardship of the land, a tangible manifestation of the belief that in giving back to the earth, we enrich not just our gardens, but our lives and the planet itself. Through composting, we participate in a cycle of renewal that sustains us all, making each handful of black gold a small but significant triumph in the quest for a more sustainable, verdant world.

The Impact of Pesticides on Human Health: A Closer Look

Pesticides, designed to protect crops from pests, weeds, and diseases, have been a cornerstone of modern agriculture for decades. While their use has contributed significantly to increasing food production and ensuring food security, growing evidence points to the adverse health consequences associated with exposure to these chemicals. The impact of pesticides on human health is complex and multifaceted, affecting individuals directly involved in their application, as well as the broader population through environmental exposure and residues found on food.

Acute Health Effects of Pesticide Exposure

Short-term, or acute, exposure to pesticides can lead to immediate health problems, which are often the result of direct contact with these chemicals during their application or accidental ingestion. Symptoms of acute pesticide poisoning can range from mild to severe and may include:

- **Skin and eye irritation**: Contact with certain pesticides can cause dermatitis, rashes, and chemical burns. Eye exposure can lead to conjunctivitis and other forms of irritation.
- **Respiratory problems**: Inhalation of pesticide vapors, mists, or dust can cause coughing, chest tightness, and shortness of breath. In severe cases, it may lead to respiratory distress or failure.
- **Nervous system effects**: Many pesticides are neurotoxic and can cause a range of neurological symptoms, including headaches, dizziness, nausea, and in severe cases, seizures, and loss of consciousness.
- **Gastrointestinal issues**: Ingesting pesticides can cause vomiting, diarrhea, abdominal pain, and in extreme cases, can damage the lining of the gastrointestinal tract.

Chronic Health Consequences

The long-term health effects of pesticides are more insidious and can manifest years after exposure. These effects are particularly concerning for individuals with chronic, low-level exposure, such as farm workers, and people living near agricultural areas. Chronic health consequences include:

- **Cancer**: Research has linked pesticide exposure to several types of cancer, including lymphoma, leukemia, brain, breast, and prostate cancer. The International Agency for Research on Cancer (IARC) has classified some pesticides as probable or possible human carcinogens.

- **Neurological disorders**: Long-term exposure to certain pesticides has been associated with an increased risk of neurological conditions, such as Parkinson's disease and Alzheimer's disease. Pesticides can affect the nervous system by disrupting neurotransmitter function and causing brain damage.

- **Reproductive and developmental effects**: Some pesticides can interfere with hormone function, leading to reproductive issues such as infertility, miscarriages, and birth defects. Exposure during pregnancy can also impact fetal development, leading to cognitive deficits and developmental delays in children.

- **Endocrine disruption**: Many pesticides are known endocrine disruptors, meaning they can interfere with the body's hormone systems. This interference can lead to a range of health problems, including obesity, diabetes, thyroid disorders, and hormone-related cancers.

Environmental Exposure and Indirect Health Effects

Beyond direct exposure, pesticides can also affect human health indirectly through environmental contamination. Pesticides can leach into groundwater and contaminate drinking water sources, leading to widespread exposure. Additionally, residues on fruits and vegetables can pose health risks to consumers, particularly children, who are more sensitive to the toxic effects of these chemicals.

The persistence of certain pesticides in the environment can lead to bioaccumulation and biomagnification, where these chemicals concentrate in the tissues of organisms higher up the food chain, including humans. This accumulation can increase the risk of chronic health effects over time.

Mitigating the Health Risks of Pesticides

Addressing the health consequences of pesticide use requires a multi-faceted approach:

- **Promoting Integrated Pest Management (IPM)**: IPM strategies focus on using a combination of biological, cultural, physical, and chemical methods to control pests, reducing the reliance on chemical pesticides.
- **Supporting organic farming**: Organic farming practices eschew synthetic pesticides, relying instead on natural pest control methods and promoting biodiversity to maintain healthy ecosystems.
- **Enhancing regulations and monitoring**: Strengthening regulations on pesticide use, including banning or restricting the use of the most harmful chemicals, and improving monitoring of pesticide residues in food and the environment can protect public health.
- **Educating and protecting workers**: Providing training on safe pesticide use, ensuring proper personal protective equipment (PPE) is used, and implementing health monitoring for agricultural workers can reduce the risk of acute and chronic health effects.

The health consequences of pesticide exposure underscore the need for a cautious and informed approach to their use. By prioritizing safer alternatives, enhancing regulatory frameworks, and raising awareness about the risks and safe practices, it's possible to mitigate the health impacts of pesticides while still meeting the demands of global food production.

PREPARING YOUR BEDS: TECHNIQUES AND TIPS

In the orchestra of gardening, preparing your beds is akin to tuning the instruments before the concert begins. It's a foundational step that sets the stage for the symphony of growth and bounty that follows. This meticulous preparation is not just about turning soil; it's a rite of passage for every gardener, a time-honored ritual that connects us to the very essence of growth. Let's delve into the techniques and tips that transform this task from mere dirt-shuffling to an art form, ensuring your garden is poised for its most productive season yet.

Understanding Your Canvas

Before a single seed is sown, take a moment to really see your garden. Observing your garden's unique conditions—the light, the shade, the way water flows (or pools)—is crucial. These observations guide you in creating a bed that complements nature's tendencies, not fights against them. It's about working *with* the land, molding your vision in harmony with its character.

The Initial Clearing

Clearing your garden bed is the first physical step in this journey. Whether you're reclaiming a neglected plot or refreshing a seasoned bed, removing weeds and debris is crucial. But take heart; even the most overgrown garden is a treasure trove of potential. As you clear, do so with a gentle hand, preserving the life that enriches the soil—worms, beneficial insects, and microorganisms. It's a cleansing process that not only clears the land but sets a clear intention for the season ahead.

Soil Analysis: Know Before You Grow

Before you break ground, understanding your soil type is imperative. Sandy, clay, loam—each has its quirks, its needs. A simple soil test, available at most garden centers, can reveal a world beneath your feet. It's not just about nutrient levels but pH balance, drainage, and texture. This knowledge is power—the power to tailor your amendments and interventions to what your soil truly needs, not just what conventional wisdom suggests.

The Art of Double Digging

Double digging, while labor-intensive, is a transformative technique for new beds. This age-old method involves removing the top layer of soil to a depth of about a foot, then loosening the layer beneath before replacing the topsoil, incorporating organic matter as you go. It's akin to giving your garden a deep-tissue massage, relieving compaction, and aerating the soil to encourage deep, healthy root growth. This method is especially beneficial in areas with poor drainage or compacted soil, laying a foundation that will pay dividends for years to come.

Enriching Your Soil

With the canvas cleared and the soil loosened, it's time to enrich. Compost, that black gold we've already discussed, is your best friend here. Spread a generous layer over your bed, working it into the top few inches of soil. This isn't just about nutrients; it's about life. Compost introduces a vibrant community of microorganisms into your garden, creating a living soil that feeds and protects your plants.

But compost isn't the only player in this game. Depending on your soil test results, you might add other organic amendments—bone meal for phosphorus, green sand for potassium, or lime to adjust ph. The key is balance, creating a nutrient-rich, well-drained foundation that encourages vigorous growth.

Shaping Your Beds

Now, with the soil prepared, it's time to shape your beds. Raised beds, whether built with wood, stone, or simply mounded soil, offer distinct advantages—improved drainage, easier access, and a barrier to some pests. But even flat beds can be delineated and designed for efficiency and beauty. Paths should be wide enough to comfortably navigate, beds narrow enough to reach the center without stepping on the soil, preserving its structure.

The Final Touch: Mulching

With your beds prepared and shaped, a final touch awaits: mulching. A layer of organic mulch—straw, wood chips, or leaf mold—can conserve moisture, suppress weeds, and gradually enrich the soil as it decomposes. It's the finishing stroke on your masterpiece, a protective blanket that keeps the soil life vibrant and vigorous.

Watering Wisdom

Watering your newly prepared beds before planting helps settle the soil and ensures it's adequately moist for seeds or seedlings. Water deeply but gently, using a rain nozzle or soaker hose to avoid erosion or compaction. This initial watering is a baptism of sorts, awakening the soil and calling forth life from its depths.

The Dance of Planting

With your beds prepared, enriched, and watered, the dance of planting begins—a dance of potential, of life waiting to unfold. Whether you're sowing seeds directly or transplanting seedlings, do so with a sense of ceremony, of gratitude for the cycle of growth you're entering into. Each seed, each plant, is a promise—a promise of nourishment, of beauty, of connection to the earth.

Ongoing Bed Maintenance

Even after planting, bed preparation continues in the form of ongoing maintenance. Keep an eye on moisture levels, mulch condition, and soil health. Your garden is a living system, and your role is that of caretaker, guiding and nurturing it through the seasons.

Reflection and Rotation

Finally, as the season progresses, reflect on the success and challenges of your garden beds. Which plants thrived? Where did challenges arise? This reflection is crucial for next season's bed preparation, informing crop rotation and adjustments in your approach. Gardening is a cycle, a never-ending quest for harmony with the land. In essence, preparing your garden beds is more than just a set of tasks; it's a philosophy, a way of engaging with the world. It's about creating a space where life can flourish, guided by your hand but governed by the inherent wisdom of nature. As you embark on this journey, remember that each step, from clearing to planting, is an act of creation, a collaboration with the earth that nurtures us all. Your garden beds are the foundation of this partnership, a testament to the care, knowledge, and love you invest in the soil. Here, in these carefully prepared beds, lies the promise of abundance, the joy of growth, and the beauty of life in its myriad forms.

SOIL AMENDMENTS FOR OPTIMAL GROWTH

In the grand tapestry of gardening, soil is the canvas upon which we paint our green aspirations. Yet, not all soil is created equal, and therein lies the gardener's challenge and opportunity. Soil amendments are the palette of nutrients and textures we use to transform this canvas, enriching and adjusting our soil to create the optimal environment for plant growth. This journey into soil amendments isn't just about adding what's missing; it's about understanding and respecting the delicate balance of nature's own design.

The Philosophy of Amendments

Soil amendments go beyond mere fertilization. They're about improving the soil structure, enhancing its water-holding capacity, and boosting its nutrient content. This holistic approach ensures that our gardens are not just surviving but thriving, embodying a harmony between the earth and the plants it hosts.

Organic Matter: The Heartbeat of Healthy Soil

At the core of soil amendments lies organic matter, the lifeblood of fertile, vibrant soil. Organic matter, such as compost, leaf mold, or well-rotted manure, introduces a complex world of microorganisms, nutrients, and minerals to the soil. It improves the soil structure, making clay soils more aerated and sandy soils better at retaining moisture.

Compost: The Universal Amendment

Compost, the gardener's gold, is perhaps the most significant amendment you can introduce to your soil. Rich in nutrients and microorganisms, it is a balanced, slow-release provider of organic matter that builds soil structure and fertility. Incorporating compost into your garden beds annually rejuvenates the soil, supporting robust plant growth and enhancing the garden's resilience to pests and diseases.

Mulches: The Protective Layer

While not a direct amendment to the soil structure, mulches play a crucial role in maintaining soil health. Organic mulches, such as straw, wood chips, or shredded leaves, break down over time, adding organic matter to the soil, conserving moisture, and suppressing weeds. They act as a buffer between the soil and the elements, moderating temperature fluctuations and protecting the soil's microcosm.

Enhancing Nutrient Content: The Balancing Act

Beyond organic matter, specific amendments target the soil's nutrient balance. The choice of amendment depends on the needs of your soil, as determined by a soil test.

- **For nitrogen**, a critical element for leafy growth, consider adding blood meal or fish emulsion. These organic sources release nitrogen slowly, feeding your plants over time without the risk of burn associated with synthetic fertilizers.
- **Phosphorus** is essential for root and flower development. Bone meal and rock phosphate are excellent organic sources, providing a slow release of phosphorus to the soil.
- **Potassium**, vital for overall plant health and disease resistance, can be supplemented with greensand or kelp meal. These amendments not only supply potassium but also trace elements that support plant growth.

Adjusting Soil pH: Creating the Ideal Environment

Soil pH profoundly affects plant growth by influencing the availability of nutrients. Most vegetables thrive in slightly acidic to neutral soil (pH 6.0 to 7.0). If your soil test reveals a pH outside this range, amendments can help adjust it:

- **To raise the pH** (in acidic soils), apply garden lime. Lime also adds calcium, beneficial for plant cell structure.
- **To lower the pH** (in alkaline soils), elemental sulfur or organic mulches like pine needles can gradually acidify the soil.

The Role of Minerals: Beyond NPK

While nitrogen, phosphorus, and potassium (NPK) get most of the attention, plants also need a suite of micronutrients and minerals to thrive. Amendments like azymite, a rock dust, supply trace minerals that can boost plant health and yield. Epsom salts, another beneficial amendment, provide magnesium and sulfur, essential for chlorophyll production and enzyme function.

The Practice of Amendment: Timing and Technique

The best time to amend your soil is before planting in the spring or after harvest in the fall. This timing allows the amendments to integrate and interact with the soil, stabilizing before planting begins.

Incorporating amendments requires a gentle hand and a thoughtful approach. Over-amending can be as detrimental as not amending at all. Follow the recommendations based on your soil test, and apply amendments evenly, working them into the top 6 to 8 inches of soil. This integration helps ensure that the amendments are accessible to your plants' root systems.

Listening to the Soil: A Continuous Dialogue

Soil amendment is not a one-time task but an ongoing conversation with your garden. Observing plant health, monitoring soil conditions, and performing regular soil tests can guide your amendment strategy, ensuring that your soil remains vibrant and life-sustaining.

The Ethos of Amendments: Nurturing the Soil as a Living Entity

In the end, amending soil is about nurturing the ground beneath our feet as a living, breathing entity. It's a commitment to stewardship, to enhancing the soil's inherent vitality without overpowering its natural rhythms. As gardeners, we're not just growing plants; we're cultivating an environment where life in all its forms can flourish.

Soil amendments are our tools in this noble endeavor, enabling us to sculpt the garden of our dreams from the soil up. They remind us that gardening is both a science and an art, a blend of knowledge, intuition, and respect for nature's wisdom. Through thoughtful amendment, we create a foundation for abundance, a garden that nourishes the body, soothes the soul, and enriches the earth.

CONCLUSION

As we draw the curtains on this journey through the heart of vegetable gardening, from the tender stirrings of soil preparation to the triumphant harvests that crown our labor, it becomes clear that gardening is much more than a mere act of cultivation. It's a profound dialogue with the earth, a testament to the resilience of life, and a celebration of the cycles that sustain us. Through the seasons, with hands in the soil and faces turned toward the sun, we've not just grown vegetables; we've nurtured a deeper connection to the planet we share and the community we build around us.

Gardening is an act of faith, a leap into the unknown, trusting that from the smallest seeds, abundant life will spring forth. It's a practice of patience, learning to move with the rhythms of nature rather than imposing our will upon it. Each chapter of this book has been a stepping stone, guiding you from the foundational knowledge of soil and plant care to the intricate dance of planning and cultivation that leads to a garden's success. Yet, beyond the practical advice and techniques shared, lies a greater truth— a reminder of our place within the web of life and our role as stewards of the earth.

The garden is a microcosm of the world, a place where the challenges we face—be it climate change, biodiversity loss, or food security—find both reflection and resolution on a scale we can touch and transform. By choosing to garden organically, to nurture biodiversity, and to sow seeds of heirloom varieties, we make a stand for sustainability and resilience. We contribute to a food system that is healthier, more equitable, and kinder to our planet.

But the journey doesn't end here. As any seasoned gardener will tell you, the garden is a teacher, offering lessons in humility, perseverance, and wonder with each passing season. There will be triumphs, moments of sheer awe at the bounty nature provides from such simple beginnings. And there will be challenges, times when pests, weather, or disease test our resolve and our resourcefulness. Yet, it is through facing these challenges that we grow, not just as gardeners but as individuals and as a community.

As you close this book and step back into your garden, remember that you carry with you not just the knowledge contained within these pages but a legacy. A legacy of gardeners who have tilled the earth before you, who have saved seeds, shared harvests, and passed down the wisdom of the soil through generations. You are part of this legacy now, a custodian of the earth and its bounty.

So, I invite you to see your garden not just as a plot of land but as a canvas for creativity, a sanctuary for biodiversity, and a foundation for community. Let it be a place where you can find solace, inspiration, and joy. Share your harvests, exchange seeds and stories with neighbors, and build a community rooted in the love of gardening and the respect for nature.

In conclusion, the journey of vegetable gardening is an ever-unfolding path, rich with the potential for learning, growth, and connection. It's a path that leads us not just back to the soil but forward to a future where gardens and the principles they teach us play a crucial role in shaping a more sustainable, compassionate world. Let us walk this path with intention and joy, for in every seed sown, there is hope for a greener, more bountiful tomorrow.

Thank you for joining me on this journey. May your gardens flourish, and may the lessons they teach enrich your life and the world around you. Here's to the gardeners—past, present, and future—and to the earth that sustains us all. Happy gardening.

Book 3: Planning Your Garden for Year-Round Bounty

In the grand tapestry of life, a garden stands as a testament to the cyclical dance of seasons, each turn of the wheel bringing with it a new face of beauty, a new array of bounty. The dream of a year-round garden, lush and thriving through the whisper of winter, the glow of summer, and the transitions of spring and fall, is a vision that captures the heart of every gardener. It's a dream that speaks to the very essence of our connection to the earth—a desire not just to witness the cycles of life but to be an active participant in them. This dream, however, is not realized by mere chance. It is the fruit of thoughtful planning, a deep understanding of the rhythms of nature, and a dedication to the art of gardening.

As we embark on the journey of **Planning Your Garden for Year-Round Bounty**, we delve into the strategies that make this dream a reality. This chapter is not merely a guide; it is an invitation to embrace your garden as a living, breathing entity that, with the right care and foresight, can offer sustenance and beauty every day of the year. It is a call to weave together knowledge, intuition, and a dash of creativity to create a garden that is not only a source of food but a sanctuary of life, regardless of the season.

Embracing the Seasons

The foundation of a year-round garden lies in an intimate understanding of the seasons—not just the four broad strokes painted by the calendar but the subtle nuances that characterize your specific piece of earth. Each region, each garden, dances to its own rhythm, and mastering this dance requires a gardener to be part observer, part choreographer. We'll explore how to tune into the unique seasonal cues of your garden, using this knowledge to select plants that will thrive in your microclimate, creating a symphony of growth that plays throughout the year.

The Canvas of Your Garden

Every garden is a canvas, and the design you choose is the first step in painting a picture of year-round abundance. This section delves into the principles of garden design that support a continuous harvest, from the structure of permanent beds to the flexibility of rotating crops. We'll discuss how to create a layout that accommodates the changing needs of your garden through the seasons, using design not just for aesthetic pleasure but as a tool for maximizing productivity and sustainability.

A Symphony of Crops

Achieving a year-round garden is akin to orchestrating a symphony, with each plant playing its part in the unfolding melody of the seasons. This section introduces the concept of successive planting and crop rotation, strategies that ensure your garden remains vibrant and productive, from the first tender greens of spring to the hearty roots of winter. We'll explore how to select a diverse palette of crops that, when harmonized, provide a continuous flow of harvests, nourishing both the body and the soul.

Extending the Season

The magic of a year-round garden often lies in the ability to extend the natural growing season. Innovations such as cold frames, greenhouses, and row covers are the tools that make this possible, acting as time machines that transport your garden beyond the constraints of the calendar. This section is a guide to the practical applications of season extenders, offering you the knowledge to push the boundaries of what's possible in your garden, bringing the dream of year-round bounty into the realm of reality.

The Pulse of Life: Water, Soil, and Companions

At the heart of every thriving garden are the elements that sustain life: water, soil, and the relationships between plants. This part of our journey focuses on how to manage these critical resources and relationships throughout the year. From the art of water conservation to the science of soil health and the practice of companion planting, we'll cover the techniques that keep your garden's pulse strong and steady, supporting a vibrant ecosystem where life flourishes in every season.

A Tapestry of Beauty and Bounty

A year-round garden is more than a source of food; it's a tapestry woven from the threads of beauty, biodiversity, and resilience. This section celebrates the garden as a habitat that supports not just human life but a host of other creatures, from the pollinators that sip nectar from your flowers to the earthworms that tunnel through your soil. We'll explore how to create a garden that is a refuge for wildlife, a place where the mutual benefits of beauty and biodiversity are realized in full.

Harvest and Celebration

Finally, the essence of a year-round garden culminates in the harvest—a time of celebration and gratitude. This section is a reflection on the rewards of your labor, offering guidance on how to harvest, store, and preserve your bounty, ensuring that the gifts of your garden are enjoyed to their fullest. It's a reminder that each meal sourced from your garden is a feast of connection, a tangible link to the earth that sustains us.

As we embark on this journey of **Planning Your Garden for Year-Round Bounty**, let us do so with open hearts and curious minds, ready to embrace the challenges and delights that each season brings. This chapter is more than a blueprint for gardening; it's a manifesto for living in harmony with the natural world, a guide to creating a garden that nourishes on every level. So, with hands in the soil and eyes to the sky, let us begin the work of crafting a garden that is a testament to the enduring cycle of life, a garden that offers bounty and beauty every day of the year.

GARDEN DESIGN AND LAYOUT STRATEGIES

In the realm of gardening, the design and layout of your garden is not merely about aesthetics; it is the bedrock upon which the year-round bounty is built. A well-thought-out garden design takes into account the unique challenges and opportunities of each season, ensuring that your garden not only survives but thrives throughout the year. This sub-chapter delves into the strategies that can transform your garden into a resilient, productive space, harmonizing with nature's cycles to yield an endless harvest.

Embracing the Garden's Microclimate

Every garden has its microclimate, influenced by factors such as sunlight, wind, and topography. Understanding your garden's microclimate is crucial. Observe the patterns of sunlight and shade throughout the year, noting areas that remain sunny even in winter, or spots that are prone to frost pockets. Design your garden layout to take advantage of these microclimates, planting sun-loving crops in the brightest

spots and using shaded areas for greens that prefer a respite from the summer heat.

The Canvas of Perennial Plantings

Perennial plants are the backbone of a year-round garden. Asparagus, artichokes, and perennial herbs not only provide yearly harvests but also define the structure of your garden. Consider their placement carefully; once established, perennials will occupy their spot for years. Use them to create permanent pathways, borders, or as anchor points around which seasonal plantings can rotate.

Succession Planting and Crop Rotation

Succession planting and crop rotation are dynamic elements of garden design. By staggering the planting of crops, you can ensure a continuous harvest. Planting a new batch of lettuce every two weeks, for example, extends the salad season far beyond the yield of a single planting. Crop rotation, on the other hand, prevents the depletion of soil nutrients and interrupts the cycles of pests and diseases. Plan your garden layout with these rotations in mind, creating spaces that can easily adapt to the changing seasons and the needs of different crops.

Integrating Raised Beds and Containers

Raised beds and containers offer versatility in garden design. They warm up faster in the spring, extending the growing season, and can be filled with soil tailored to specific crop needs. Raised beds also improve drainage, reducing the risk of root rot in wet seasons. Containers are invaluable for urban gardeners or those with limited space, enabling gardening on patios or balconies. They can be moved to optimize sunlight exposure or to protect tender plants from frost. Integrate these elements into your garden design to maximize your growing potential.

Utilizing Vertical Space

Vertical gardening is a game-changer for maximizing yield, especially in small gardens. Trellises, walls, and fences can support climbing plants like beans, peas, and cucumbers, freeing up precious ground space for other crops. Vertical structures can also provide shade for heat-sensitive plants or act as windbreaks, protecting tender vegetables from harsh conditions.

The Role of Water Management

Efficient water management is integral to garden design. Consider the placement of rain barrels to capture water for irrigation, and design your garden layout to facilitate water access. Drip irrigation systems, strategically placed, ensure that water is delivered directly to the root zone of plants, minimizing waste and preventing disease.

Paths and Access

Design your garden with access in mind. Paths should be wide enough to navigate comfortably, allowing for the passage of wheelbarrows or garden carts. They should also be designed to minimize soil compaction around plants, using materials like mulch or gravel that allow water to percolate through.

Planning for Pollinators and Beneficial Insects

A garden buzzing with life is a sign of health and productivity. Design your garden to attract pollinators and beneficial insects by including a variety of flowering plants. Lavender, borage, and marigold not only add beauty to the garden but also support a healthy ecosystem that keeps pest populations in check.

Adapting to the Seasons

A garden designed for year-round bounty must be adaptable. Incorporate structures like cold frames or hoop houses into your design, which can be used to extend the growing season by protecting plants from frost. Consider also the winter landscape; deciduous trees and shrubs can provide wind protection in winter while allowing sunlight through when they are leafless in the spring.

Reflecting and Recording

Finally, a successful garden design is an evolving one. Keep a garden journal, recording what works and what doesn't, noting how the garden changes through the seasons. This reflective practice allows you to adapt and refine your garden design over the years, tailoring it more closely to the unique rhythm of your gardening year. Designing a garden for year-round bounty is both an art and a science. It requires observation, creativity, and a willingness to experiment and adapt. By considering the unique needs of each season, embracing the dynamics of succession planting and crop rotation, and creating a flexible, resilient garden layout, you can enjoy the fruits of your labor every day of the year. This journey of garden design is not just about the harvests you reap but about deepening your connection to the land and the cycles of nature.

SEASONAL PLANTING GUIDES

Crafting a garden that yields a bounty through all seasons is akin to conducting an orchestra: each plant, with its unique rhythm and timing, must come together in harmony. This sub-chapter is your guide to the symphony of seasonal planting, ensuring that every note is played at the right moment, creating a continuous melody of growth and harvest in your garden.

Spring: The Awakening

As the frost recedes and the soil warms, spring beckons with promise. It's the season to sow seeds of hope, both literally and metaphorically.

- **Early Spring**: Begin with cool-season crops that can withstand a little chill in the air. Lettuces, peas, spinach, and radishes can be sown directly into the soil as soon as it's workable. It's also time to plant potatoes and onions sets, heralding the first hearty harvests to come.

- **Mid to Late Spring**: As the threat of frost diminishes, broaden your planting to include beets, carrots, and leeks. This is also the moment to start your warm-season crops indoors—tomatoes, peppers, and eggplants—preparing them for the balmy days ahead.

Summer: The Time of Abundance

Summer is the crescendo in the garden's year, a time of vibrant growth and generous yields.

- **Early Summer**: Transition to warmth-loving plants as the last frost date passes. Cucumbers, squash, beans, and corn thrive in the lengthening days. It's also the ideal time to transplant those tomatoes, peppers, and eggplants started indoors, allowing them to bask in the full strength of summer's sun.

- **Mid to Late Summer**: While enjoying the fruits of your labor, don't forget to look ahead. Sow fall crops like kale, turnips, and broccoli. Consider a second planting of beans or a late sowing of carrots for a late-season harvest.

Fall: The Harvest Season

As the heat of summer softens into the milder days of fall, the garden offers up its most bountiful harvests.

- **Early Fall**: Continue to harvest summer crops, while beginning to sow cool-season greens like spinach and arugula under the protection of a cold frame or fleece. It's also time to plant garlic for next year's harvest.

- **Late Fall**: As the garden winds down, plant cover crops such as clover or vetch. These will protect and enrich the soil over the winter, keeping it alive and active even as the garden rests.

Winter: The Quiet Preparation

Winter might seem like a time of dormancy, but it's an essential period of rest and preparation for both the garden and the gardener.

- **Early Winter**: Harvest the last of the fall crops and winter-hardy greens. Apply mulch to perennial beds for protection against the cold.

- **Mid to Late Winter**: This is the season of planning and anticipation. Order seeds and start certain crops indoors—onions and leeks require a long growing season and benefit from an early start. Reflect on the past year and adjust your garden plans for the coming season.

The Continuous Cycle: Succession Planting

To achieve a year-round bounty, embrace the practice of succession planting. By staggering plantings of certain crops every few weeks, you ensure a continuous harvest. Lettuces, radishes, and greens are ideal for this technique, offering fresh flavors every few weeks.

Crop Rotation: The Guardian of Soil Health

Rotate your crops annually to prevent the build-up of pests and diseases and to avoid depleting the soil of specific nutrients. Divide your garden into sections, rotating each crop family (nightshades, legumes, brassicas, etc.) through the sections over a three or four-year cycle. This practice not only protects your garden but can also improve soil structure and fertility.

Tuning Into Nature's Rhythms

Understanding your garden's microclimate is crucial for seasonal planting. Pay attention to the first and last frost dates but also to the unique conditions of your garden. A sheltered spot might allow you to push the boundaries of the season, while a colder pocket might require extra protection for early or late crops.

The Symphony of Perennials

While annuals play the melody of the seasonal garden, perennials provide the baseline. Asparagus, rhubarb, berries, and fruit trees offer reliable harvests year after year. Integrate these into your garden design, considering their long-term location and needs.

The Art of Extension

To truly master year-round bounty, explore the art of season extension. Cold frames, greenhouses, and hoop houses can protect crops from early frosts, allowing you to harvest well into the colder months. Similarly, shade cloth and careful watering can extend the life of cool-season crops into the warmer months.

Reflection and Adaptation

A garden is a living, breathing entity, constantly changing and evolving. What works one year might need adjustment the next. Keep a garden journal, recording what you plant and when, noting successes and areas for improvement. This reflective practice is invaluable, guiding you to refine and perfect your garden's harmony.

Embracing the rhythm of the seasons, understanding the unique melody of your garden, and conducting the symphony of crops through thoughtful planning and adaptation, you can achieve a garden that sings with life and bounty all year round. This dance with the seasons, this partnership with the earth, is the essence of gardening—a journey of continuous discovery, renewal, and abundance.

SUCCESSION PLANTING AND CROP ROTATION

In the ever-evolving tapestry of the garden, two practices stand as pillars of sustainability and productivity: succession planting and crop rotation. Together, they form a dynamic strategy that maximizes yield, maintains soil health, and minimizes pest and disease pressures. This sub-chapter delves into how these practices can be seamlessly woven into the fabric of your garden planning, ensuring a lush, productive garden throughout the year.

The Rhythm of Succession Planting

Succession planting is akin to the art of keeping the dance floor alive, ensuring that as one song ends, another begins without missing a beat. It's the practice of planting crops in a way that extends the harvest season, either by staggering plantings of a single crop or by planting a new crop after one has been harvested.

- **Staggered Plantings**: This involves sowing seeds or planting seedlings at regular intervals, rather than all at once. For crops like lettuce, radishes, and green beans, staggered plantings every two weeks can provide continuous harvests throughout their growing season.
- **Sequential Cropping**: After harvesting a crop, immediately replant the space with another crop that will mature in the remaining part of the growing season. For example, following early spring peas with summer squash or planting fall garlic in the space left by summer tomatoes.

- **Interplanting**: Grow fast-maturing crops between rows or alongside slower-growing crops. Radishes or spinach can be planted between rows of carrots or parsnips, utilizing space efficiently and being harvested before the slower crops need room to expand.

Crop Rotation: The Guardian of the Garden

Crop rotation is the practice of not planting the same crop, or crops from the same family, in the same location for at least three years. This ancient technique is rooted in wisdom, safeguarding the soil from depletion and breaking the life cycles of pests and diseases.

- **A Four-Year Plan**: A simple rotation plan involves dividing your garden into at least four sections and rotating crops among these sections each year. A basic rotation might move crops through sections in the following order: leafy greens and legumes, followed by nightshades, then roots and bulbs, and finally brassicas.
- **Benefits Beyond Pest Control**: Rotation improves soil structure and fertility. Different crops have different nutrient needs and root depths, which can help prevent nutrient depletion and compaction, enhancing soil health over time.
- **Companion Planting Integration**: Consider companion planting within your rotation plan. Certain crop combinations can enhance growth, deter pests, or improve flavor, adding another layer of sophistication to your garden's design.

Implementing Succession and Rotation

To bring succession planting and crop rotation into your garden, a thoughtful approach and good record-keeping are essential.

1. **Start with a Plan**: Before the season begins, sketch your garden layout and decide on the crops you wish to grow. Map out your succession and rotation strategies, taking into account the needs and timings of different crops.
2. **Keep Records**: Maintain a garden journal or logbook. Note what was planted where and when, including succession plantings and the results. This record becomes invaluable over the years as you refine your strategies.
3. **Be Flexible**: Weather, pests, and other unforeseen challenges will arise. Be prepared to adjust your plans, replanting or rotating crops as necessary to respond to these challenges.

Advanced Techniques for Year-Round Bounty

- **Overlapping Seasons**: With careful planning, you can overlap seasons for a year-round harvest. Use cold frames, greenhouses, or mulches to protect late-season crops and start early spring crops under cover.
- **Catch Crops**: Utilize the concept of catch crops—fast-growing plants sown between longer-term crops. These can be harvested before they compete significantly for space, light, or nutrients.
- **Green Manures**: In your rotation plan, include periods where a section of the garden is sown with green manures—crops grown not for harvest, but to be turned into the soil to improve its structure and nutrient content.

Embracing Nature's Cycles

The essence of succession planting and crop rotation lies in their respect for nature's inherent cycles. These practices are not just techniques for maximizing production; they are expressions of a deep understanding of and respect for the natural world. They embody the principles of giving back to the earth and of taking only what we need, when we need it.

In the garden, every action is a part of a larger cycle of life, death, renewal, and regrowth. Succession planting and crop rotation are tangible manifestations of these cycles, a dance with the earth that nourishes not just our bodies with fresh produce throughout the year but also our spirits with the deep satisfaction of working in harmony with nature.

Through thoughtful planning and a commitment to these practices, gardeners can achieve not just a year-round bounty but a sustainable, vibrant garden ecosystem. This is the garden as a microcosm of the world we wish to see: diverse, resilient, and abundantly alive.

PERENNIAL VEGETABLES FOR YEAR-ROUND HARVESTS

In the orchestra of the garden, perennial vegetables are the deep, resonant tones that provide continuity and stability. They're the steadfast friends you can count on year after year, offering not just sustenance but a backbone around which the rest of your garden dances. Perennials challenge the annual cycle of sowing, growing, and harvesting, offering a sustainable, low-maintenance cornerstone for a year-round bounty.

The Perennial Philosophy

Embracing perennials in your garden is more than a planting strategy; it's a philosophical shift. It's about looking beyond the immediate gratification of annual harvests to the long-term rewards of a garden that grows in complexity and productivity with each passing year. Perennials, with their deep roots, improve soil structure, enhance water retention, and draw up nutrients from the depths, enriching the soil surface for their annual companions.

The Core Perennials

While the world of perennial vegetables might seem uncharted to many gardeners, it's rich with variety and flavor. Here are some stalwarts of the perennial vegetable garden:

- **Asparagus** (*Asparagus officinalis*): Spearheading the spring garden, asparagus rewards patience with bountiful harvests for 20 years or more after a few seasons of establishment.
- **Rhubarb** (*Rheum rhabarbarin*): A harbinger of spring, rhubarb's tart stalks are a delight in pies and preserves. A well-tended rhubarb patch can produce for a decade.
- **Artichokes** (*Cynara scolymus*): These architectural plants offer both beauty and bounty, with their large, edible flower buds ready for harvest in late summer.
- **Horseradish** (*Armoracia rusticana*): With its fiery roots, horseradish adds spice to the garden and the table. Once established, it requires minimal care and offers annual harvests.
- **Sorrel** (*Rumex acetous*): This leafy green thrives in the cooler months, offering a lemony tang to salads and soups. Its early spring growth provides greens when most gardens are still waking.

Integrating Perennials into the Garden

Perennials require a thoughtful approach to integration, as their permanent nature means they'll occupy their space for years. Consider the following when planning your perennial plantings:

- **Location**: Choose a spot where they can grow undisturbed, away from areas that will be dug over for annual crops.
- **Companions**: Plant perennials with compatible companions that share similar water and nutrient needs, ensuring a harmonious garden ecosystem.
- **Soil Preparation**: Invest in preparing the soil deeply, enriching it with compost and ensuring good drainage, as perennials will tap into this foundation for many years.

Year-Round Harvests with Perennials

To truly leverage perennials for year-round harvests, diversity is key. Including a range of perennials ensures that, as one plant's season ends, another begins. For example, pair early-spring asparagus with summer-harvested artichokes and fall-flourishing Jerusalem artichokes (*Helianthus tuberoses*), creating a seamless transition through the seasons.

Maintenance and Care

Perennial vegetables, while low-maintenance, do benefit from periodic care:

- **Mulching**: Apply a generous layer of organic mulch annually to suppress weeds, retain soil moisture, and add nutrients.
- **Pruning**: Some perennials, like rhubarb, benefit from removing spent flowers to encourage leaf growth.
- **Division**: Many perennials, such as asparagus and horseradish, can become crowded. Periodic division helps maintain vigor and provides new plants to expand your garden or share.

Perennials for Problem Areas

Perennials can also solve garden challenges. Plants like sea kale (*Crambo maritima*) and lovage (*Levisticum officinale*) thrive in tough conditions, from salty winds to poor soil, making them ideal for challenging garden spots where annuals might struggle.

The Hidden Gems

Beyond the well-known perennials, there are hidden gems waiting to be discovered by adventurous gardeners:

- **Good King Henry** (*Chenopodium bonus-Henrico's*): An old-fashioned favorite, offering spinach-like leaves and edible flower buds.
- **Skirret** (*Sium sesamum*): Produces sweet, crunchy roots that were a delicacy in medieval Europe.
- **Turkish Rocket** (*Bunias orientalism*): Offers spicy, broccoli-like buds and is drought-resistant once established.

The Perennial Impact

Incorporating perennial vegetables into your garden is more than a pathway to year-round harvests; it's a commitment to the environment. Perennials stabilize soil, reduce erosion, and create habitats for beneficial insects and wildlife. They're a testament to the gardener's role as a steward of the land, nurturing a plot that gives back year after year.

In the end, the perennial garden is a reflection of the gardener's vision for a sustainable, productive, and beautiful space. It evolves, grows, and deepens with time, offering not just food, but a connection to the cycles of life and growth. As these perennials take root in your garden, they become more than plants; they're the enduring legacy of your care, a perennial testament to the gardener's art.

CONCLUSION

As we draw the curtains on our journey through **Planning Your Garden for Year-Round Bounty**, we find ourselves standing at the threshold of a new beginning rather than at the end of a chapter. This exploration has been more than a mere accumulation of gardening strategies; it has been a profound invitation to connect deeply with the cycles of nature, to understand the subtle nuances of our unique environments, and to cultivate a space that thrives throughout the seasons. We have ventured together through the intricacies of garden planning, the art of selecting crops for continuous harvest, and the innovative techniques for extending the growing season, each step an affirmation of the garden's potential to sustain and enchant every day of the year.

The essence of what we've explored is not just the how-tops of year-round gardening but the why's. It's about seeing the garden not as a static entity but as a living, breathing extension of ourselves—a canvas upon which the story of our interaction with the earth is painted in vibrant greens, yellows, and reds. This approach to gardening transcends the mere act of planting and harvesting; it becomes a dialogue with the land, a dance with the elements, and a testament to the resilience and abundance of nature.

The Symphony of Seasons

Embracing the garden as a year-round endeavor invites us to listen to the symphony of the seasons, each movement a different expression of life. Spring's tender beginnings, summer's lush abundance, autumn's reflective transition, and winter's quiet rest—each season contributes its unique tone to the garden's ongoing melody. This symphony does not just happen; it is the result of intentional, thoughtful planning and the gardener's willingness to be attuned to the rhythms of nature.

The Canvas of Creativity

Our gardens are canvases for creativity, places where the mundane meets the miraculous. With each seed planted, with every design decision made, we imprint part of our vision, our hopes, and our dreams onto this living tapestry. The garden in return offers us a bounty that feeds not just our bodies but our souls, providing a sanctuary of beauty and peace in a world that often moves too fast.

The Journey of Stewardship

Year-round gardening is an ongoing journey of stewardship, a commitment to caring for the land that sustains us. This stewardship is not a burden but a privilege—an opportunity to engage in the most fundamental act of nurturing life. Through the cycles of preparing, planting, tending, and harvesting, we become active participants in the stewardship of our planet, cultivating not just plants but a deeper respect and appreciation for the natural world.

The Celebration of Harvest

And at the heart of it all is the harvest—the celebration of the garden's bounty, a tangible reward for the gardener's labor and love. The act of harvesting connects us to generations of gardeners and farmers who have come before us, reminding us of the timeless cycle of life that we are a part of. This bounty is not merely measured in the quantity of produce gathered but, in the joy, and satisfaction of sharing the fruits of our labor with friends and family, of meals made more meaningful by the ingredients grown in our gardens.

Looking Forward

As we conclude this chapter and look forward to the cycles of seasons to come, let us carry forward the knowledge and inspiration gleaned from these pages. Let us approach our gardens with a renewed sense of wonder and purpose, ready to embrace the challenges and delights of planning a garden that offers year-round bounty. The journey does not end here; it evolves and continues with each seed sown, with every garden plan drafted, with the ongoing dialogue between gardener and garden.

In this dance with the seasons, in this endeavor to create spaces of abundance and beauty, we find a reflection of life itself—complex, ever-changing, and deeply enriching. So, armed with our plans, our dreams, and a commitment to stewardship, let us step into the garden, into the heart of nature, and cultivate a world that nourishes, sustains, and thrives throughout the year.

BOOK 4: PLANTING TECHNIQUES AND SEED STARTING

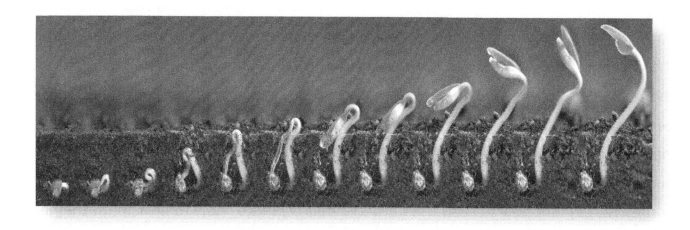

Embarking on the journey of **Planting Techniques and Seed Starting** is akin to setting sail into the vast, uncharted waters of creation itself. This chapter is not merely a collection of methods and steps; it is an odyssey into the heart of gardening, where the act of planting seeds transcends the physical. Here, we delve into the sacred ritual of bringing new life into the world, a process that mirrors the cycles of life, death, and rebirth that govern our very existence.

In the garden, every seed planted is a whisper of potential, a promise of growth, beauty, and nourishment. Yet, the path from seed to flourishing plant is one fraught with challenges and learning opportunities. It requires not just knowledge and skill, but a deep connection to the rhythms of nature and an intuitive understanding of the life we seek to cultivate.

The Alchemy of Seed Starting

The journey begins with the alchemy of seed starting, an ancient practice that turns the dormant into the vibrant. This is where we learn to coax life from the seemingly lifeless, a testament to the gardener's role as both nurturer and witness to miracles. The right combination of soil, moisture, warmth, and light sparks the magic of germination, a moment of creation that never ceases to inspire awe.

But this alchemy is not left to chance. It is a craft honed by understanding the unique needs of each seed, the specific conditions that whisper to it, "It's time to grow." We explore the soils that cradle these seeds, the vessels that house them, and the light that guides them, crafting environments that mimic the embrace of Mother Earth herself.

The Art of Planting

With the birth of seedlings, we step into the art of planting, a dance between the gardener and the garden. This section is a deep dive into the techniques that ensure these tender new lives thrive in their transition from container to earth. We discuss the nuances of direct sowing versus transplanting, the importance of timing, and the gentle care required to nurture young plants in their formative stages.

Planting is not merely about placing seeds or seedlings in the ground; it is about understanding the landscape—both visible and invisible—that will become their new home. We explore how to read the garden's microclimate, how to anticipate the needs of plants at different stages of growth, and how to create a symbiosis between the soil and the souls we plant within it.

Nurturing Growth

As our seedlings take root, we turn our attention to nurturing growth, to guiding these plants towards their fullest expression. This section is an ode to the ongoing relationship between gardener and plant, a dynamic interplay of care, observation, and adjustment. We delve into the mysteries of watering, the intricacies of feeding, and the art of pruning, each a conversation, a way of listening and responding to the silent language of plants.

The Gardener's Toolbox

In this chapter, we also open the gardener's toolbox, examining the tools and technologies that support the journey from seed to harvest. From the simplest trowel to the most advanced greenhouse setups, we consider how these tools extend our capabilities, allowing us to cultivate more effectively, more sustainably, and with greater joy.

The Philosophy of Seed Starting and Planting

Yet, beneath the practical lies the philosophical, the recognition that what we do in the garden reflects deeper truths about life itself. Seed starting and planting are acts of hope and faith, a belief in the potential for growth and renewal. They are exercises in patience and humility, reminding us that we are not the sole creators but collaborators with nature, participating in a cycle of life that predates and will outlast us.

The Tapestry of Life

Ultimately, **Planting Techniques and Seed Starting** is about weaving our own thread into the tapestry of life. It is an acknowledgment that each plant we grow is a part of a larger whole, a contributor to the garden's diversity and resilience. As gardeners, we are stewards of this tapestry, tasked with nurturing not just individual plants but the health of the ecosystem itself.

A Journey of Discovery

As we embark on this chapter, we do so as explorers, ready to discover the wonders and challenges of bringing new life into our gardens. We stand at the threshold of creation, armed with knowledge, tools, and, most importantly, a sense of wonder. Let us proceed with open hearts and curious minds, ready to learn, to grow, and to be transformed by the act of gardening.

In the pages that follow, let us journey together through the sacred acts of seed starting and planting, uncovering the techniques that will guide us towards a bountiful harvest. This is not just a chapter in a book; it is a chapter in our lives as gardeners, a chapter filled with growth, discovery, and the endless joy of creating life in harmony with the earth.

SEED SELECTION AND SAVING

The very soul of your garden begins with the seeds you choose to plant. This elemental choice is where your garden's journey starts, weaving a story from the soil to the supper table. In this sub-chapter, we'll navigate the intricacies of seed selection and the empowering practice of saving seeds, ensuring that every gardener can sow the seeds of a resilient, bountiful future.

The Art of Seed Selection

Choosing seeds is akin to choosing the characters for a play; each one plays a unique role in the garden's performance. When selecting seeds, consider these critical factors:

- **Open-Pollinated versus Hybrid**: Open-pollinated varieties, including heirlooms, have been nurtured over generations, capable of producing seeds that will grow true to type. Hybrids, on the other hand, are the result of cross-pollination between varieties, designed for specific traits like disease resistance or productivity. While hybrids can offer vigor and uniformity, their seeds might not reliably produce the same characteristics in subsequent generations.

- **Adaptation to Local Conditions**: Seeds that are adapted to your local climate and soil conditions are more likely to thrive. Look for varieties that have been grown successfully in your area, or consider participating in local seed exchanges.

- **Biodiversity**: Embrace a variety of species and varieties to enhance the ecological resilience of your garden. Biodiversity encourages a healthy, balanced ecosystem, reducing dependency on a single crop and mitigating the impact of pests and diseases.

Seed Saving: A Legacy of Growth

Saving seeds is an act of preservation; it's about saving not just a plant, but a story and a heritage. It connects us to the past and sows a legacy for future generations. Here's how to embark on the rewarding journey of seed saving:

- **Selecting Plants for Seed Saving**: Focus on saving seeds from healthy, vigorous plants that exhibit desirable traits, such as superior flavor, productivity, or disease resistance. This selection process, known as 'rouging', ensures that you carry forward the best qualities.

- **Understanding Pollination**: To save seeds that will produce true to type, it's essential to understand how your plants are pollinated. Many vegetables, especially heirlooms, are open-pollinated by wind or insects, which can lead to cross-pollination between different varieties within the same species. Strategies such as distance isolation, timing planting to avoid simultaneous flowering, or using physical barriers like row covers can help maintain purity.

- **Harvesting and Processing Seeds**: Wait until seeds are fully mature before harvesting, which often means the fruit is past its edible stage. For dry-seeded crops (e.g., beans, lettuce), allow seeds to dry on the plant before harvesting. For wet-seeded crops (e.g., tomatoes, cucumbers), seeds need to be extracted and often fermented briefly to remove the gelatinous coating, then washed and dried.
- **Storing Seeds**: Proper storage is crucial for maintaining seed viability. Store seeds in a cool, dry place, ideally in paper envelopes or glass jars. Labeling seeds with the variety name and date of collection avoids future confusion and ensures seeds are used while still viable.

Ethical Considerations and Community Engagement

Seed saving is more than a personal endeavor; it's a communal responsibility. By saving and sharing seeds, you contribute to genetic diversity and help preserve plant varieties that might otherwise be lost. Engaging with seed libraries, participating in seed swaps, and contributing to community gardens are ways to deepen your impact and connect with a network of like-minded gardeners.

The Cultural and Environmental Impact

Beyond the practical benefits, seed saving is a powerful statement in support of environmental stewardship and food sovereignty. It represents a rejection of the commodification of seeds by agribusiness, advocating instead for a system where seeds are shared freely, diversity is celebrated, and everyone has access to the genetic resources necessary for food security.

Looking to the Future

As we face the challenges of climate change and biodiversity loss, the roles of seed selection and saving have never been more critical. By choosing diverse, locally adapted seeds and engaging in seed saving, gardeners can play a vital role in creating resilient, sustainable food systems. This practice is not just about gardening; it's about cultivating a future where diversity, resilience, and community are at the heart of our relationship with the land.

In this journey from seed to harvest, every gardener holds the power to influence the landscape of tomorrow. Through thoughtful seed selection and the mindful practice of saving seeds, we ensure that our gardens—these vibrant testaments to life's persistence—are rich not only in produce but in possibilities. Let us sow these seeds with hope, nurturing them into a legacy of abundance, diversity, and resilience for generations to come.

STARTING SEEDS INDOORS

Starting seeds indoors is akin to nurturing a dream from the faintest whisper to a vibrant reality. It's an act of faith and foresight, allowing gardeners to extend the growing season and coax life from the dormant potential of seeds. This practice is not just about getting a head start on spring; it's a profound engagement with the cycle of growth, offering a front-row seat to the miracle of life. Let's explore the foundational steps to successfully start seeds indoors, transforming your home into a nursery brimming with future harvests.

Creating the Ideal Environment

The key to successful seed starting lies in replicating the optimal conditions for germination—warmth, moisture, and light.

- **Warmth**: Most seeds require a warm soil environment to germinate. Maintaining soil temperatures of 65-75°F (18-24°C) is ideal for most species. Heating mats specifically designed for seed starting can provide consistent warmth, especially in cooler climates or during late winter starts.

- **Moisture**: Seeds need to be consistently moist to germinate. Use a fine spray to moisten the soil initially, and cover your containers with plastic wrap or a humidity dome to retain moisture and warmth. Be vigilant to prevent the soil from becoming waterlogged, as this can lead to fungal diseases like damping-off.

- **Light**: Once seeds sprout, they need plenty of light to grow strong and healthy. A sunny south-facing window may suffice, but to ensure even growth without leggedness, consider using grow lights. Position the lights just a few inches above the seedlings, raising them as the plants grow.

Selecting Containers and Soil

- **Containers**: You can start seeds in almost any type of container, as long as it has drainage holes. Reuse pots, make your own from newspaper, or use peat pots or cell flats. The key is ensuring that seedlings have enough room to develop roots but are easy to transplant later.

- **Soil**: Use a light, seed-starting mix that is specifically designed to promote good air circulation and water retention. These mixes are usually sterile, helping to prevent disease from affecting your tender seedlings.

Sowing Your Seeds

- **Planting Depth**: A general rule of thumb is to plant seeds at a depth of about two times their width. Some tiny seeds need light to germinate and should be pressed gently into the soil surface instead of covered.

- **Labeling**: Always label your containers with the plant name and the date sown. This simple step can prevent a lot of confusion and help track your seedlings' progress.

Care and Maintenance

- **Watering**: Keep the soil moist but not soggy. Using a spray bottle or a watering can with a fine rose can prevent dislodging or burying the seeds.

- **Thinning**: Once seedlings develop their first true leaves, thin them out if they are too crowded. This ensures that the remaining seedlings have enough space and resources to grow strong.

- **Hardening Off**: Before transplanting seedlings outdoors, they need to be acclimated to their new environment. Begin by placing them outside in a sheltered spot for a few hours each day, gradually increasing their exposure to sunlight and outdoor temperatures over a week.

Troubleshooting Common Issues

- **Leggy Seedlings**: Seedlings that stretch towards the light are not receiving enough. Ensure that grow lights are close enough, or rotate seedlings regularly to encourage even growth.

- **Damping-Off**: This fungal disease can be devastating for seedlings. To prevent it, avoid overwatering and ensure good air circulation around your plants. Using a fan to simulate a gentle breeze can be beneficial.

Transplanting Seedlings

- **When to Transplant**: Seedlings are ready to move to their garden home when they have developed a robust set of true leaves and have been properly hardened off.
- **The Process**: Handle seedlings gently by their leaves, not their delicate stems. Make holes in the prepared garden bed, place each seedling in its hole, and gently firm the soil around it, watering well afterward.

The Joy of Seed Starting

Starting seeds indoors is not just a method to jump-start the growing season; it's a journey of connection and discovery. It allows gardeners to experiment with varieties not readily available as starts and offers the satisfaction of nurturing plants from the very beginning of their lifecycle. This hands-on engagement with the process of growth enriches our understanding of nature's rhythms and our place within them.

Through the act of seed starting, we are reminded of the potential that lies in small beginnings and the patience required to see dreams to fruition. It's a testament to the gardener's role as both caretaker and student in the endless lessons the garden provides. As these seedlings stretch towards the light, so too do we grow, learning and adapting in the pursuit of a harvest that feeds more than just our bodies. This, perhaps, is the greatest harvest of all, cultivated from the humble beginnings of seeds started within the warmth of our homes.

DIRECT SOWING AND TRANSPLANTING

Direct sowing and transplanting are two sides of the same coin, each vital to the gardener's toolkit, offering pathways to a thriving, productive garden. Direct sowing connects us to the age-old practice of planting seeds where they will grow, while transplanting nurtures young plants, preparing them for their journey from container to earth. This sub-chapter explores the nuances of each method, guiding you through their rhythms and requirements, ensuring that every plant gets the best possible start in your garden.

Direct Sowing: Embracing the Simplicity

Direct sowing is the act of planting seeds directly into the garden soil. It's a practice as old as agriculture itself, favored for its simplicity and direct connection to the earth.

- **Timing is Everything**: The key to successful direct sowing lies in understanding the right time to plant. This depends on the specific needs of each crop and the local climate, particularly the soil temperature. Frost-hardy vegetables can be sown early in the season, while heat-lovers must wait until the threat of frost has passed.

- **Preparing the Bed**: Create a welcoming bed for your seeds by ensuring the soil is loose, well-drained, and rich in organic matter. A smooth, fine seedbed allows for better seed-to-soil contact, crucial for germination.

- **Sowing Depth and Spacing**: Follow the seed packet instructions for depth and spacing. A general rule is to plant seeds at a depth twice their size. Proper spacing allows for air circulation and reduces competition for nutrients and light.

- **Water Wisely**: After sowing, water gently but thoroughly. The goal is to moisten the soil without displacing the seeds. Keep the soil consistently moist until germination.

Transplanting: A Gentle Transition

Transplanting is the process of moving a plant from its starting container into the garden. It's a critical step for plants started indoors or in a greenhouse, bridging their nurtured beginning to their independent growth in the garden.

- **The Right Time**: Transplant seedlings after they've developed their true leaves and have been hardened off. Choose an overcast day or late afternoon to minimize stress from heat and sunlight.

- **Preparing the Transplant**: Water your seedlings well before transplanting to ensure the soil sticks to the roots, reducing root disturbance.

- **Digging the Perfect Hole**: The hole should be slightly larger than the root ball of the seedling. If transplanting into a container, ensure it's large enough to accommodate the plant's growth.

- **Handling with Care**: Gently remove the seedling from its container, handling it by the leaves rather than the stem. Disturb the roots as little as possible. For peat pots, tear away the top rim to prevent wicking moisture away from the plant.

- **Settling In**: Place the seedling in the hole and backfill with soil, firming gently around the base. Water thoroughly to settle the soil around the roots and eliminate air pockets.

Aftercare for Direct Sowing and Transplanting

- **Watering**: Keep the soil moist but not waterlogged. Seedlings are particularly vulnerable to both drought and overwatering in their early stages.
- **Mulching**: Once seedlings have established, apply a layer of organic mulch to conserve moisture, suppress weeds, and regulate soil temperature.
- **Thinning**: For directly sown plants, thinning is crucial to prevent overcrowding. Do this early to minimize competition and ensure the healthiest plants have room to grow.
- **Protection**: Young plants are susceptible to pests and environmental stresses. Use row covers or plant collars to protect them from insects and extreme temperatures.

The Dance of Direct Sowing and Transplanting

Each method, direct sowing and transplanting, offers unique benefits and challenges. Direct sowing eliminates the shock of transplanting, allowing plants to grow strong from the start in their natural environment. It's ideal for root crops and fast-growing greens that thrive with minimal disturbance. Transplanting, meanwhile, extends the growing season and allows for greater control over the growing conditions during the seedling's vulnerable early days. It's perfect for slow-growing or tender plants that need a head start.

Embracing the Cycle

Whether direct sowing or transplanting, each method connects us more deeply to the cycle of growth and the rhythms of nature. They remind us of our role not just as gardeners but as stewards, nurturing each plant from seed to harvest with attention and care. This cycle of growth, from the smallest seed to the most bountiful harvest, is a journey filled with learning, challenges, and the profound satisfaction of cultivating life.

As you delve into the practices of direct sowing and transplanting, you'll find each seed, each plant, tells its own story—a narrative of resilience, adaptation, and growth. These practices are not just about producing food; they're about cultivating a relationship with the land, a dialogue with nature that teaches us about balance, patience, and the enduring beauty of growth. With each seed sown directly into the welcoming earth, with each seedling tenderly transplanted, we sow the seeds of a future both abundant and alive with possibility.

COMPANION PLANTING SECRETS

In the tapestry of the garden, plants do not live in isolation; they are part of a complex web of relationships. Companion planting taps into this natural synergy, guiding us to pair plants in ways that enhance growth, deter pests, and improve flavor. This ancient practice, rooted in observation and experience, unlocks the garden's full potential, transforming it into a vibrant ecosystem. Let's explore the secrets of companion planting, unveiling the partnerships that can lead your garden to flourish.

Understanding Companion Planting

Companion planting is the strategic placement of different plants in close proximity for mutual benefit. This method goes beyond mere aesthetics, drawing on the natural affinities between plants to create a harmonious garden environment. The benefits are manifold:

- **Pest Management**: Some plants naturally repel pests or attract beneficial insects that prey on common garden pests.
- **Pollination Support**: Planting flowers among crops can attract pollinators, enhancing the productivity of fruit and vegetable plants.
- **Nutrient Sharing**: Certain plant combinations can optimize the use of nutrients. For example, legumes fix nitrogen in the soil, which can benefit nitrogen-loving plants placed nearby.
- **Shade Regulation**: Taller plants can provide necessary shade to sun-sensitive shorter plants, creating a microclimate that supports a diverse range of crops.

The Principles of Successful Companion Planting

- **Diversity is Key**: A diverse garden is a resilient garden. By mixing crops, you mimic natural ecosystems, reducing the risk of pest infestations and diseases.

- **Know Your Plants**: Understanding the needs and characteristics of each plant is crucial. This knowledge allows you to pair plants that have compatible soil, water, and sunlight requirements.

- **Observe and Adapt**: Companion planting is not a one-size-fits-all solution. What works in one garden may not work in another. Observation and flexibility are essential to find the best combinations for your specific conditions.

Classic Companion Planting Combinations

Some companion planting partnerships have stood the test of time, celebrated for their effectiveness:

- **Tomatoes and Basil**: This classic duo not only tastes great together but planting basil alongside tomatoes can help repel pests like mosquitoes and flies, and is believed to improve the flavor of the tomatoes.

- **Carrots and Onions**: The strong scent of onions can deter carrot flies, while carrots are said to repel onion flies and aphids, making them perfect bedfellows.

- **Beans and Corn**: In a traditional Three Sisters planting, beans fix nitrogen in the soil, benefiting the nitrogen-hungry corn, while cornstalks provide a natural trellis for the beans to climb.

- **Marigolds and Just About Anything**: Marigolds are the workhorses of the companion planting world, repelling nematodes and other pests through their roots and attracting beneficial insects with their blooms.

Companion Planting for Soil Health and Beyond

Companion planting also plays a crucial role in maintaining soil health and reducing the need for chemical fertilizers and pesticides:

- **Nitrogen Fixers**: Legumes, such as beans and peas, enrich the soil with nitrogen, benefiting neighboring plants.

- **Deep and Shallow Rooters**: Pairing deep-rooted plants with shallow-rooted ones can help make efficient use of nutrients at different soil levels, reducing competition and enhancing soil structure.

Companion Planting Myths and Misconceptions

While companion planting offers numerous benefits, it's important to approach it with a critical eye. Not all claimed benefits are backed by science, and what works in one garden's unique conditions may not work in another. Experimentation and observation are key to discovering what works best for you.

Implementing Companion Planting in Your Garden

- **Start Small**: Experiment with a few companion planting pairs to observe their effects before fully integrating this approach into your garden.
- **Keep Records**: Documenting what combinations, you try and their outcomes can be incredibly helpful for refining your companion planting strategy over time.
- **Think Beyond Pest Control**: While deterring pests is a significant benefit, consider companion planting for its ability to enhance pollination, improve soil health, and even increase yields.

The Future of Companion Planting

As we face the challenges of sustainable gardening and agriculture, companion planting stands out as a practice that aligns with ecological principles, promoting biodiversity, reducing reliance on chemical inputs, and fostering a deeper connection with the natural world. Its principles remind us that in the garden, as in life, relationships matter. Through careful observation and thoughtful implementation, companion planting can turn our gardens into thriving ecosystems, abundant with life and yield.

In the end, companion planting is not just about planting certain crops together; it's about cultivating a philosophy of harmony, balance, and interdependence. It teaches us that every plant, every creature in the garden has a role, a purpose, and a place in the tapestry of life. By unlocking these secrets, we unlock the full potential of our gardens, creating spaces that are not only productive but also resilient, sustainable, and in tune with the rhythms of the natural world.

CONCLUSION

As we draw to a close on our exploration of **Planting Techniques and Seed Starting**, it's evident that we've traversed much more than mere methodology.

We've embarked on a journey that intertwines the practical with the philosophical, grounding ourselves in the rich soil of gardening wisdom while reaching towards the sunlit ideals of nurturing life. This chapter has not only equipped us with the tools and knowledge to begin our gardens from the very genesis of a seed but has also instilled in us a profound appreciation for the intricate dance of creation that gardening embodies.

In delving into the alchemy of seed starting, we've unraveled the mysteries hidden within the humble seed, learning to coax life from dormancy with a blend of science and intuition. This process, while often challenging, has revealed itself as a testament to the resilience of nature and the power of patient, attentive care. We've seen how a tiny, inert seed holds within it the potential for abundant life, waiting for the right conditions to unfurl into vibrant growth.

Transitioning from seed to seedling, we ventured into the art of planting, learning to gently integrate our tender charges into the broader canvas of our gardens. This step, critical in the life cycle of a plant, bridges the gap between controlled environment and the wild, unpredictable nature of the outside world. Through this, we've gleaned the importance of timing, technique, and the deep connection that forms between gardener and plant during this intimate act of transplantation.

Moreover, we've explored the gardener's toolbox, uncovering the practical aspects of nurturing our nascent gardens. From the simplest of tools to the most complex systems, we've learned that each serves not just a functional purpose but is an extension of our intentions and care towards the garden. These tools enable us to cultivate more efficiently and effectively, yet they also remind us of our place within the larger ecosystem, as stewards rather than conquerors.

Throughout this chapter, a recurring theme has been the profound relationship between the gardener and the garden—a dynamic, evolving interplay that extends beyond the physical acts of planting and tending. We've seen how the garden serves as a mirror, reflecting back at us not only the fruits of our labor but the growth within ourselves. Gardening, especially at the stage of seed starting and planting, is an exercise in hope, patience, and humility, teaching us lessons of resilience, care, and the interconnectedness of all life.

In conclusion, **Planting Techniques and Seed Starting** stands as more than a guide; it is a meditation on the act of creation itself. It celebrates the garden as a locus of continuous discovery, a space where the cyclical nature of life is expressed in the most vivid and tangible forms. As we move forward, armed with the knowledge and insights gleaned from this chapter, we are reminded that each garden we cultivate is a testament to our participation in the ongoing dance of life.

Each seed we plant is a vote of confidence in the future, an act of faith in the unseen and a commitment to the stewardship of the earth that sustains us. So, let us carry forward the lessons learned, the inspiration found, and the connections forged. Let us step into our gardens with a renewed sense of purpose and possibility, ready to nurture the seeds of today into the bountiful harvests of tomorrow. In every seed lies the potential for growth, and in every gardener, the potential to bring forth life from the earth. This is the essence of gardening, a journey of endless cycles, discoveries, and the joyful labor of love that connects us deeply to the natural world.

BOOK 5: WATER, MULCH, AND FERTILIZATION

In the symphony of the garden, water, mulch, and fertilization are the essential notes that harmonize to sustain life. This chapter delves into the art and science of providing your garden with the nourishment it needs, crafting a delicate balance that fosters growth and vitality. Water, the lifeblood of the garden, is more than just a necessity—it's a resource to be wielded with wisdom and care, ensuring that every drop contributes to the flourishing of your plants. Mulch, the garden's protective blanket, not only conserves moisture and suppresses weeds but also enriches and insulates

the soil, creating a thriving environment for microbial life. Fertilization, when approached with an understanding of the garden's unique needs, offers the targeted nutrients that plants crave, tailored to support their growth through every stage of development.

Together, these three elements form a trinity of garden care, each supporting the other in a sustainable cycle of growth. Learning to master these practices means moving beyond mere gardening into the realm of stewardship, where each action is taken with mindfulness of its impact on the garden ecosystem. This chapter is your guide to navigating these crucial aspects of garden care, blending practical advice with insights into creating a garden that is not only productive but resilient and vibrant. As we explore the nuances of water, mulch, and fertilization, we unlock the secrets to a garden that thrives in harmony with nature, yielding bounty and beauty in abundance.

In the tapestry of gardening, water, mulch, and fertilization are the threads that bind the garden's health, vitality, and productivity. **Water, Mulch, and Fertilization** delves into these foundational elements, each a pillar that supports the lush landscape we dream of cultivating. This chapter isn't just a compilation of techniques; it's a deeper exploration of how these essential practices intertwine with the natural rhythms of the earth, embodying a gardener's commitment to nurturing life in its most verdant form.

Water: The Essence of Vitality

Water, the essence of all life, is as vital to our gardens as it is to our own bodies. Learning to wield water wisely is a dance with nature itself, where too much or too little can tip the scales away from harmony. We'll explore the art of irrigation, balancing the garden's thirst with the need for conservation, and how to tailor watering practices to the unique needs of each plant. This section aims to imbue gardeners with a sense of reverence for water, encouraging practices that sustain both the garden and the broader environment.

Mulch: The Garden's Protector

Mulch is the garden's protector, a simple yet profound ally in the quest for a balanced ecosystem. Beyond its ability to retain moisture and regulate soil temperature, mulch serves as a guardian against erosion, a deterrent to weeds, and a slow-releasing supplier of nutrients. We'll dive into the selection and application of mulch, revealing how this seemingly modest layer is pivotal in creating a garden that is resilient and self-sustaining.

Fertilization: Nourishing the Roots of Growth

Fertilization is the act of feeding the garden, but it goes far beyond merely providing nutrients. It's about understanding the soil's and plants' needs, creating a cycle of nourishment that supports not just growth but health. From organic composts to carefully chosen amendments, this section examines how to fertilize in harmony with nature, enriching the soil in ways that benefit the current garden and generations of gardens yet to come.

As we embark on this journey through **Water, Mulch, and Fertilization**, we do so with the understanding that these elements are not just tasks to be checked off a list. They are expressions of care, reflections of the gardener's role as a steward of the earth. With each chapter, we're not just cultivating plants; we're cultivating a deeper connection to the garden, to the environment, and to the cycle of life itself. Let's step forward with mindful intention, ready to nurture our gardens with the wisdom, respect, and love they, and the world around us, truly deserve.

EFFICIENT WATERING PRACTICES

In the realm of gardening, water is both a giver of life and a mirror reflecting our relationship with the natural world. Efficient watering practices are not just about quenching the thirst of our plants; they embody our commitment to stewardship, conservation, and the mindful management of vital resources. This sub-chapter explores the art and science of watering, guiding you through methods that ensure your garden thrives while fostering a sustainable harmony with the environment.

Understanding Your Garden's Water Needs

The first step towards efficient watering is understanding the unique water needs of your garden. Various factors influence these needs, including plant type, soil composition, climate, and the life stage of your plants. Recognizing these factors allows you to tailor your watering practices, ensuring that each plant receives just the right amount of water—no more, no less.

The Timing of Watering

- **Morning is Prime Time**: Watering in the early morning minimizes evaporation, allowing water to penetrate deeply into the soil. It also gives leaves a chance to dry out during the day, reducing the risk of fungal diseases.

- **Evening Considerations**: While evening watering is better than the heat of the day, it can leave plants damp overnight, increasing disease risk. If evenings are your only option, aim to water the soil directly, avoiding the foliage.

Techniques for Efficient Watering

- **Soaker Hoses and Drip Irrigation**: These systems deliver water directly to the soil, minimizing waste and reducing evaporation. They're ideal for maintaining consistent soil moisture and are particularly beneficial in vegetable beds and perennial borders.

- **Rainwater Harvesting**: Collecting rainwater in barrels or cisterns for garden use is an excellent way to reduce demand on municipal water systems and make use of a free resource. Plants also benefit from rainwater's natural, soft quality.

- **Mulching**: A generous layer of organic mulch helps retain soil moisture, reducing the frequency of watering needed. Mulch acts as an insulating blanket, keeping the soil cool and moist.

Watering Wisely

- **Deep Watering**: Encourage deep root growth and drought tolerance by watering deeply and less frequently. This practice helps plants become more resilient and efficient in water use.

- **Observation and Adjustment**: Regularly check the moisture level of your soil to tailor your watering schedule to actual need rather than sticking rigidly to a timetable. Adjust based on rainfall and temperature changes.

- **Container Considerations**: Potted plants have different watering needs than ground-planted ones. Ensure containers have adequate drainage and check them more frequently, as they can dry out quickly.

Avoiding Common Watering Pitfalls

- **Overwatering**: More is not always better. Overwatering can lead to root rot, nutrient leaching, and unhealthy plant growth. Learn to recognize the signs of overwatering and adjust accordingly.
- **Uneven Watering**: Ensure even coverage throughout your garden to prevent dry spots and water stress. Sprinkler systems should be checked regularly for coverage and adjusted as plants grow.

The Impact of Soil on Watering

The type of soil in your garden greatly affects its water-holding capacity and, consequently, your watering practices.

- **Sandy Soils**: These drain quickly and may require more frequent, light watering to maintain moisture.
- **Clay Soils**: Water slowly and deeply, as clay soils hold water longer and are prone to surface runoff if watered too quickly.
- **Loam Soils**: Ideal for gardening, loam retains moisture well and allows for moderate, consistent watering practices.

Advanced Watering Strategies

- **Olla Irrigation**: An ancient method that involves burying unglazed terracotta pots filled with water near plants. The water seeps out slowly, providing a steady moisture source directly to the roots.
- **Hydro zoning**: Grouping plants with similar water needs together can make watering more efficient and reduce water waste.

Fostering a Water-Wise Garden

Efficient watering extends beyond technique; it's about creating a garden that inherently requires less water.

- **Choosing Drought-Resistant Plants**: Native plants and those adapted to dry conditions can significantly reduce the water needs of your garden.
- **Improving Soil Health**: Incorporating organic matter into your soil improves its water retention and drainage, making your garden more drought-resilient.
- **Garden Design**: Designing your garden with water conservation in mind, such as through the use of swales and rain gardens, can naturally enhance moisture availability to plants.

The Ripple Effect of Efficient Watering

By adopting efficient watering practices, gardeners can play a pivotal role in conserving water, a resource that's becoming increasingly precious in many parts of the world. Beyond the immediate benefits to our gardens, these practices contribute to a larger ethos of sustainability and respect for our planet's natural resources.

Efficient watering is not just a set of techniques; it's a philosophy that intertwines respect for nature with the practical aspects of gardening. It reminds us that each action we take, each drop of water we use, is part of a larger cycle of life that sustains us all. As we tune our gardens to the rhythms of this cycle, we nurture not just our plants but the very world that cradles them.

MULCHING FOR WEED CONTROL AND MOISTURE RETENTION

Mulching, a practice as ancient as gardening itself, serves as a guardian of the soil, a keeper of moisture, and a barrier against the relentless advance of weeds. This sub-chapter delves into the art and science of mulching, revealing how a simple layer of organic or inorganic material on the soil's surface can profoundly influence the health and productivity of your garden. Through mulching, we create a microcosm of the forest floor, emulating nature's method of conserving moisture, enriching the soil, and suppressing unwanted growth.

The Magic of Mulch

Mulch performs several critical functions in the garden:

- **Moisture Retention**: By covering the soil, mulch reduces evaporation, keeping the soil moist for longer. This not only conserves water but ensures that plants have a steady supply of moisture, even in the heat of summer.
- **Weed Suppression**: A thick layer of mulch can inhibit weed germination and growth, reducing the need for manual weeding. Without light, weed seeds struggle to sprout, and those that do are easily pulled from the loose mulch layer.

- **Temperature Regulation**: Mulch acts as an insulating layer, protecting the soil from extreme temperature fluctuations. In summer, it keeps the soil cool; in winter, it can protect plant roots from freezing.
- **Soil Improvement**: Organic mulches gradually decompose, adding valuable organic matter to the soil. This improves soil structure, enhances nutrient availability, and encourages the activity of beneficial soil organisms.

Choosing Your Mulch

The choice of mulch can vary depending on the needs of your garden, the plants you're growing, and the goals you wish to achieve:

- **Organic Mulches** include straw, grass clippings, shredded leaves, bark, and wood chips. They enrich the soil as they decompose but may need to be replenished annually.
- **Inorganic Mulches**, such as gravel, pebbles, and black plastic, do not improve soil fertility but can be more effective at suppressing weeds and conserving moisture over the long term.

Applying Mulch Effectively

- **Timing**: Apply mulch in late spring, after the soil has warmed up. Mulching too early can slow soil warming and plant growth.
- **Thickness**: A layer of 2-4 inches is generally recommended. Too little may not effectively suppress weeds or conserve moisture, while too thick a layer can impede water infiltration and suffocate roots.
- **Clearing the Area**: Before mulching, remove existing weeds and water the soil thoroughly. This creates the optimal starting conditions for your plants to thrive.
- **Avoiding the Stem**: When mulching around plants, leave a small space around the base of each plant. This prevents moisture buildup around the stems, reducing the risk of rot and disease.

Special Considerations

- **Mulching Vegetables and Annuals**: These plants benefit significantly from organic mulches, which warm the soil and break down over the growing season, feeding the soil. Straw is particularly favored in vegetable gardens for its lightness and ease of removal at season's end.

- **Perennials and Trees**: For these, a more permanent mulch like wood chips or bark may be appropriate. These materials break down slowly, offering long-term benefits to the soil and plants.

The Ecological Benefits of Mulching

Beyond its immediate benefits to the garden, mulching is a practice with profound ecological implications. By reducing the need for frequent watering, mulching conserves water—a precious and often scarce resource. The suppression of weeds through mulching minimizes the reliance on chemical herbicides, contributing to a healthier, more sustainable garden ecosystem. Furthermore, the use of organic mulches supports the cycle of life in the garden, feeding the soil and fostering a vibrant community of earthworms, microbes, and fungi.

Troubleshooting Common Mulching Challenges

- **Nitrogen Depletion**: Some organic mulches, particularly those high in carbon like straw and wood chips, can temporarily deplete soil nitrogen as they decompose. To counteract this, consider adding a nitrogen-rich fertilizer or compost beneath the mulch.
- **Pest Harborage**: While mulch can support beneficial soil life, it can also provide shelter for pests. Regularly inspect mulched areas and manage pests through natural or mechanical means to prevent problems.
- **Mold and Fungus**: In wet climates, some mulches can harbor mold or fungus. Choosing the right type of mulch and ensuring proper application thickness can help mitigate these issues.

Mulching as a Philosophy

At its heart, mulching embodies a philosophy of gardening that respects and emulates natural processes. It teaches us patience, as we wait for organic mulches to decompose and enrich the soil. It instills in us a sense of stewardship, as we use mulching to protect and nurture the soil that sustains our plants. And it reminds us of the interconnectedness of all things, as we observe the cycle of life, death, and rebirth that unfolds in the mulch-covered garden.

Incorporating mulching into your gardening practices is not just a technique for weed control and moisture retention; it's an embrace of a more sustainable, attentive, and ecologically mindful way of gardening. Through the simple act of spreading mulch, we connect with the deeper rhythms of the natural world, creating gardens that are not only productive but also resilient, diverse, and beautifully in tune with the earth.

Organic Fertilizers and How to Use Them

In the rich tapestry of the garden, organic fertilizers are the threads that add depth and vibrancy, feeding the soil and nurturing the plants with the full spectrum of nutrients they crave. Moving beyond the quick fix of synthetic fertilizers, organic options offer a sustainable, slow-release source of nutrients, building soil health and supporting the complex web of life below the surface. This sub-chapter delves into the world of organic fertilizers, guiding you through their benefits, types, and application techniques to enrich your garden naturally.

The Essence of Organic Fertilizers

Organic fertilizers are derived from natural sources, including plants, animals, and minerals. Unlike their synthetic counterparts, they provide more than just nutrients; they enhance soil structure, increase water retention, and encourage beneficial microbial activity. This holistic approach to fertilization nurtures plants over the long term, fostering vigorous growth and resilience to pests and diseases.

Types of Organic Fertilizers

- **Animal-Based**: Blood meal, bone meal, fish emulsion, and manure are rich in essential nutrients like nitrogen, phosphorus, and potassium. They break down slowly, providing a steady supply of nutrients.
- **Plant-Based**: Compost, seaweed, cottonseed meal, and green manure are excellent sources of organic matter and nutrients. They not only feed plants but also improve soil health and biodiversity.
- **Mineral-Based**: Greensand, rock phosphate, and lime supply trace minerals and help balance soil pH, making nutrients more available to plants.

Application Techniques

The key to using organic fertilizers effectively lies in understanding the specific needs of your garden and the nature of the fertilizers themselves.

- **Testing the Soil**: Before applying any fertilizer, conduct a soil test. This will reveal which nutrients are lacking and guide your choice of fertilizer.
- **Timing**: Early spring is an ideal time to apply organic fertilizers, giving plants a nutrient boost at the start of the growing season. Some fertilizers, like compost, can be applied any time, as they primarily improve soil structure and fertility.
- **Application Methods**:
  - **Broadcasting**: Spread the fertilizer evenly over the soil surface and gently work it into the soil. This method is suitable for area-wide applications, especially before planting.
  - **Side-Dressing**: Apply fertilizer around the base of growing plants, supplying nutrients directly where they're most needed. This is particularly effective for heavy feeders and mid-season boosts.
  - **Foliar Feeding**: Diluted liquid fertilizers, like fish emulsion or seaweed extract, can be sprayed directly onto plant leaves. This method provides a quick nutrient uptake, beneficial for stressed or rapidly growing plants.

Understanding the Nutrients

- **Nitrogen (N)** is crucial for leafy growth and green color. Animal-based fertilizers are typically high in nitrogen.
- **Phosphorus (P)** supports root development, flowering, and fruiting. Bone meal is an excellent phosphorus source.
- **Potassium (K)**, found abundantly in greensand and wood ash, enhances overall plant health and disease resistance.

The Benefits of Going Organic

- **Sustainability**: Organic fertilizers are renewable, biodegradable, and less likely to contribute to environmental pollution.
- **Soil Health**: They improve soil structure and promote a diverse ecosystem of beneficial organisms, leading to healthier plants and higher yields.
- **Safety**: Being natural products, they are safer for the environment, gardeners, and consumers, reducing the risk of chemical exposure.

Complementing with Compost

While not a fertilizer in the strict sense, compost deserves special mention for its unparalleled role in enriching the garden. It provides a balanced array of nutrients, improves soil structure, and introduces beneficial microorganisms. Regular additions of compost can significantly reduce the need for other fertilizers, making it the cornerstone of any organic fertilization strategy.

Troubleshooting Common Issues

- **Slow Release**: Organic fertilizers generally release nutrients slowly, which is beneficial for long-term plant health but may not quickly correct severe deficiencies.
- **Odor**: Some organic fertilizers, especially those animal-based, can have a strong odor when first applied, though this usually dissipates quickly.
- **Variable Nutrient Levels**: Because they are natural products, the nutrient levels in organic fertilizers can vary. It's important to adjust application rates based on observation of plant growth and health.

Embracing the Organic Philosophy

Using organic fertilizers is more than a gardening tactic; it's an embrace of a philosophy that values sustainability, soil health, and the long-term wellbeing of the planet. It reflects a commitment to gardening in a way that supports the earth's natural cycles and conserves its resources for future generations.

Incorporating organic fertilizers into your garden practice nourishes not just your plants but the entire garden ecosystem, from the smallest soil microbe to the tallest tree. This approach creates a garden that is not only productive but also vibrant, resilient, and deeply connected to the rhythms of the natural world. Through the thoughtful use of organic fertilizers, we step into harmony with nature, cultivating gardens that are a testament to the beauty and abundance of the earth.

NATURAL GROWTH ENHANCERS

In the lush tapestry of the garden, every gardener seeks that elusive thread of vitality that will transform their garden from simply surviving to vibrantly thriving. Natural growth enhancers, derived from the very essence of nature, are that thread. Beyond the basics of water, mulch, and fertilization, there exists a realm of organic elixirs, beneficial microbes, and natural amendments that can elevate the health and productivity of your garden. This sub-chapter unveils the secrets of these natural growth enhancers, guiding you to harness their power in your pursuit of a garden that not only grows but flourishes.

Embracing the Power of Compost Tea

Compost tea, a liquid gold brewed from the decomposition of organic matter, is more than just a fertilizer; it's a vibrant, living concoction teeming with beneficial microorganisms. When applied to soil or foliage, compost tea acts as both a plant nutrient and a protector against diseases, invigorating your garden with every drop.

- **Brewing the Perfect Batch**: At its core, brewing compost tea involves steeping quality compost in water, often with the addition of aeration and sometimes organic catalysts to encourage microbial growth. The result is a potent, microbe-rich tea that can be applied directly to your garden's soil or leaves.

Harnessing the Benefits of Mycorrhizae

Mycorrhizae, a symbiotic relationship between fungi and plant roots, is a natural enhancer of plant growth. These fungi extend the root system's reach, enabling better water and nutrient absorption, enhancing plant resilience against stress, and improving soil structure.

- **Inoculating Your Garden**: Incorporating mycorrhizal fungi into your garden is simple. Many nurseries sell mycorrhizae as a powder or granules that can be sprinkled into planting holes or mixed with seed-starting mediums. This one-time application can have lasting benefits throughout the life of your plants.

The Role of Beneficial Insects

Beneficial insects, nature's own pest control agents, play a crucial role in a healthy garden ecosystem. Encouraging a diverse population of these insects can significantly reduce pest populations naturally.

- **Attracting Beneficials**: Planting a variety of flowering plants, especially those with umbrella-shaped flowers like dill and yarrow, can attract beneficial insects.

Providing habitats, such as insect hotels, further encourages their presence in your garden.

Seaweed Extracts: The Ocean's Gift

Seaweed extracts, packed with minerals, growth hormones, and trace elements, offer a comprehensive boost to plant health. They can stimulate root development, enhance resistance to pests and diseases, and promote vigorous growth.

- **Application Methods**: Seaweed extracts are available in liquid form or as a powder that can be dissolved in water. They can be applied as a foliar spray or directly to the soil, offering flexibility in how you deliver their benefits to your plants.

Using Rock Dust for Trace Minerals

Rock dust, finely ground rocks rich in minerals, can replenish soils depleted of trace elements, leading to healthier, more nutrient-dense plants.

- **Application and Benefits**: Sprinkling rock dust over your garden beds and incorporating it into the soil can slowly release essential minerals, enhancing plant growth and fruit and vegetable quality over time.

Wood Ash: A Source of Potassium and Lime

Wood ash from untreated wood can be a source of potassium and lime, beneficial for many garden plants. It can raise soil pH, making it particularly useful for sweetening acidic soils.

- **Cautious Use**: Because wood ash can significantly alter soil pH, it should be used sparingly and only after a soil test to determine your garden's needs.

The Magic of Mulching with Alfalfa

Alfalfa, whether as hay, meal, or pellets, is not just for mulch. It's a growth enhancer, packed with nitrogen, vitamins, and minerals, and it even stimulates beneficial soil microbes.

- **Unlocking Alfalfa's Potential**: Use alfalfa as a base for homemade compost, a direct mulch, or steep it into a nutrient-rich tea to water your plants or foliar feed them.

Molasses: Feeding the Soil Microbes

Molasses, a sweet treat for soil microbes, can boost the microbial activity in your garden soil, translating into improved nutrient availability and absorption for your plants.

- **Molasses in the Garden**: Adding molasses to your compost tea or watering regime can invigorate the soil life, enhancing soil structure and fertility.

The Wisdom of Using Eggshells and Coffee Grounds

Eggshells and coffee grounds, often discarded as kitchen waste, are treasures in the garden. Eggshells provide calcium, crucial for preventing blossom end rot in tomatoes and peppers, while coffee grounds add organic matter and nitrogen to the soil.

- **Practical Application**: Crush eggshells and sprinkle them around the base of your plants or add them to your compost pile. Coffee grounds can be mixed into the soil or composted, but should be used in moderation due to their acidity.

The Holistic Approach to Garden Vitality

Natural growth enhancers embody the holistic approach to gardening, where every element of the garden ecosystem is considered and nurtured. It's a strategy that goes beyond mere plant growth, aiming to foster a garden that is not only productive but also vibrant and resilient.

- **A Cycle of Symbiosis**: By implementing these natural growth enhancers, you participate in a cycle of symbiosis, where each element of your garden supports and is supported by others. This cycle, rooted in the principles of organic and sustainable gardening, ensures that your garden is a thriving, self-sustaining ecosystem.

The Garden as a Reflection of the Gardener

The use of natural growth enhancers is a testament to the gardener's dedication to nurturing life in its most pure and sustainable form. Each choice, from brewing compost tea to inviting beneficial insects, reflects a commitment to gardening practices that honor the earth and its abundance.

As we explore and implement these natural growth enhancers, we weave a richer, more vibrant tapestry in our gardens. It's a tapestry that tells a story of care, respect, and a deep, enduring connection to the natural world. In this story, the garden is not just a space for cultivation but a sanctuary of growth, learning, and harmony with nature.

CONCLUSION

As we draw the curtains on our exploration of **Water, Mulch, and Fertilization**, we find ourselves not at the end of a mere chapter but at the beginning of a more nuanced, deeper understanding of gardening's fundamental elements. These pillars—each essential in its own right—form the backbone of a thriving, vibrant garden. But beyond the practical knowledge and techniques shared, this chapter has been an invitation to engage more deeply with the rhythms of nature, to cultivate a garden that is not only productive but also a steward of the earth's resources.

Water: A Renewed Perspective

Our journey began with water, the lifeblood of the garden, and it's here we've learned the art of balance. Through smarter irrigation techniques and a deeper appreciation for conservation, we emerge with a renewed perspective on how to nurture our plants while respecting the finite nature of this vital resource. This understanding propels us toward practices that ensure our gardens are oases of sustainability, mirroring the natural world's efficiency and abundance.

Mulch: The Unsung Hero

Mulch, the garden's unsung hero, has revealed itself as much more than a mere layer on the soil surface. It's a multifaceted tool that protects, nurtures, and sustains. The insights gained about the types, benefits, and strategic uses of mulch encourage us to see it as an integral component of the garden ecosystem, one that offers protection and nourishment to our plants while significantly reducing our environmental footprint.

Fertilization: The Art of Feeding

Fertilization has unfolded as the art of feeding not just the plants but the soil itself. We've navigated the complexities of nutrients and soil health, recognizing that a well-fed garden is the cornerstone of growth and vitality. This section has equipped us with the knowledge to enrich our gardens thoughtfully and responsibly, fostering a cycle of life that supports not only the current season's harvest but the sustainability of future gardens.

In conclusion, **Water, Mulch, and Fertilization** has been more than a guide; it has been a journey towards a more mindful, intentional form of gardening. As we move forward, let's carry with us the lessons of stewardship, balance, and respect for the natural world. Let's continue to nurture our gardens with care, wisdom, and a deep appreciation for the intricate web of life they support. Through mindful application of water, strategic use of mulch, and thoughtful fertilization, we not only enhance our own gardens but contribute to the health and well-being of the planet. Here's to the gardens we cultivate and the legacy we leave in the soil for generations to come.

BOOK 6: INTEGRATED PEST AND DISEASE MANAGEMENT

In the garden, a delicate balance reigns between growth and decay, bounty and loss. Integrated Pest and Disease Management (IPDM) is the gardener's strategy for maintaining this balance, a holistic approach that respects the complexities of the natural world. This chapter delves into the art and science of managing pests and diseases through understanding, prevention, and careful intervention, aiming not for eradication but for equilibrium.

IPDM is about observing the garden's ecosystem, identifying potential threats before they become problems, and using a variety of tactics to bolster the garden's defenses. It's a method that prioritizes the health of the soil, the resilience of plants, and the preservation of beneficial insects alongside the targeted management of pests and diseases. By embracing IPDM, gardeners can cultivate spaces that are not only productive but also vibrant, diverse, and sustainably managed.

This chapter will guide you through the foundations of IPDM, from the early detection of pests and diseases to the selection of resistant plant varieties and the implementation of cultural, biological, and, when necessary, chemical controls. It will also explore the importance of fostering biodiversity in the garden, encouraging a natural balance that can deter pests and diseases before they take hold.

Through the principles of IPDM, we learn that every challenge in the garden is an opportunity for growth—not just for the plants, but for the gardeners who tend them. It's a journey of continual learning, observation, and adaptation, leading to gardens that are not only more resilient but also more in harmony with the world around them.

Embarking on **Integrated Pest and Disease Management**, we step into a realm where the gardener becomes both protector and steward, engaging in a delicate dance with the natural world. This chapter is not merely a guide to warding off pests and diseases; it's an exploration of how to cultivate resilience and harmony within the garden ecosystem. Here, we embrace the philosophy that every challenge in the garden is an opportunity for growth—not just for our plants but for ourselves as gardeners.

In the world of gardening, pests and diseases are often viewed as adversaries, but this chapter invites you to see them through a different lens. These challenges are part of the natural cycle, indicators of the garden's health and balance. Integrated Pest and Disease Management (IPDM) is about more than just control; it's about understanding the underlying causes of these issues and addressing them in a way that strengthens the garden's natural defenses.

A Foundation in Prevention

At the heart of IPDM lies the principle of prevention. We'll delve into practices that build a strong foundation for garden health, from selecting disease-resistant plant varieties to fostering biodiversity that encourages beneficial insect populations. These proactive measures set the stage for a garden where balance is maintained, and challenges are met with resilience.

Identifying Friends and Foes

Learning to identify the garden's allies and adversaries is crucial. This section will equip you with the knowledge to discern between beneficial insects and those that pose a threat, understanding the roles they play in the garden's ecosystem. We'll explore how to encourage natural predators and use barriers and traps effectively, all while minimizing harm to the garden's helpers.

The Art of Organic Intervention

When intervention is necessary, we turn to organic and least-toxic solutions, prioritizing the garden's long-term health over quick fixes. This chapter offers strategies for employing organic pesticides, homemade remedies, and cultural practices that mitigate pest and disease pressures. Each technique is chosen with care, ensuring that the garden remains a vibrant, life-supporting space.

As we navigate **Integrated Pest and Disease Management**, remember that each decision we make affects not just the immediate wellbeing of our plants but the broader environment. This chapter is a journey towards becoming more thoughtful, observant gardeners, armed with the knowledge to protect our gardens in a way that honors the intricate web of life they support. Let's step forward with a commitment to stewardship, ready to cultivate gardens that are not only productive but resilient and in harmony with the natural world.

IDENTIFYING COMMON PESTS AND DISEASES

The garden is a microcosm of life, a place where the cycles of growth and decay unfold before our eyes. Within this verdant realm, pests and diseases are not mere intruders but part of the intricate web of life that challenges us to cultivate resilience and balance. This sub-chapter embarks on the essential task of identifying common pests and diseases that gardeners may face, arming you with the knowledge to recognize early signs and respond with wisdom.

The Art of Observation

Before diving into specifics, cultivate the art of observation. Regularly walking through your garden, inspecting the underside of leaves, and noting changes in plant health are practices as crucial as watering and weeding. Early detection is key in managing pests and diseases, often making the difference between a minor issue and a widespread problem.

Common Garden Pests

- **Aphids**: Tiny, sap-sucking insects that cluster on new growth and undersides of leaves, often accompanied by sticky "honeydew." Leaves may curl or yellow, and growth can be stunted.
- **Spider Mites**: Microscopic pests that weave fine webs on the undersides of leaves, causing yellow speckling. Severe infestations can lead to leaf drop and plant death.
- **Japanese Beetles**: Metallic blue-green beetles that feast on a wide range of plants, skeletonizing leaves and devouring flowers.
- **Slugs and Snails**: These nocturnal mollusks leave a slimy trail and irregular holes in leaves, favoring moist, shaded gardens.
- **Cabbage Worms**: Velvety green larvae that devour brassicas, leaving large, ragged holes in leaves.

Common Plant Diseases

- **Powdery Mildew**: A fungal disease recognizable by white, powdery spots on leaves and stems. It thrives in both humid and dry conditions, affecting photosynthesis and plant vigor.

- **Early Blight and Late Blight**: These fungal diseases attack tomatoes and potatoes, causing dark, concentric spots on leaves and fruit. Late blight can also produce a white, fuzzy growth on the underside of leaves.

- **Rust**: Identified by its namesake rust-colored pustules on the undersides of leaves, this fungal disease can weaken plants significantly.

- **Black Spot**: Common on roses, this fungal disease manifests as black spots surrounded by yellowing foliage, leading to leaf drop.

- **Verticillium and Fusarium Wilts**: Soil-borne fungal diseases that cause yellowing, wilting, and death of leaves, starting from the bottom of the plant. They can decimate susceptible crops like tomatoes and cucumbers.

Tools for Identification

- **Garden Journals**: Keeping a detailed record of observations, including photographs and notes on symptoms, can help track the progress of pests and diseases.

- **Extension Services**: Local extension services and master gardener programs are invaluable resources for identification and management strategies.

- **Online Databases and Apps**: Many online resources and apps offer databases of pests and diseases, complete with images and treatment suggestions.

Integrated Management Strategies

Once pests or diseases are identified, integrated management strategies prioritize ecological balance and minimal harm. These strategies include:

- **Cultural Controls**: Practices such as crop rotation, selecting resistant varieties, and maintaining healthy soil can prevent or mitigate outbreaks.

- **Physical and Mechanical Controls**: Barriers, traps, and manual removal can effectively manage pests without resorting to chemicals.

- **Biological Controls**: Encouraging or introducing natural predators and beneficial insects offers a sustainable way to keep pest populations in check.

- **Chemical Controls**: Used as a last resort, organic and least-toxic pesticides should be applied judiciously, with attention to timing and potential impacts on non-target organisms.

The Ethos of Integrated Pest and Disease Management

Embracing integrated pest and disease management is not about seeking a garden free from any challenge but about fostering a space where ecological balance reigns. It's a commitment to observing, understanding, and intervening in ways that honor the complex interdependencies of life. This approach nurtures not only healthier plants but also a deeper connection to the natural world, where every gardener becomes a steward of the land.

In identifying common pests and diseases, we arm ourselves with knowledge, the most potent tool in the gardener's kit. With this knowledge, we're prepared to face challenges not with fear or frustration but with the confidence that comes from understanding. We learn to see pests and diseases not as enemies but as indicators, guiding us toward a more attentive, responsive, and ultimately sustainable practice of gardening.

ORGANIC PEST CONTROL SOLUTIONS

In the quest for harmony within the garden, the use of organic pest control solutions stands as a testament to the gardener's dedication to sustainability and environmental stewardship. These methods, derived from nature's own defenses, offer a way to manage pest populations without resorting to harsh chemical pesticides, thus protecting our gardens, our health, and the planet. This sub-chapter explores a variety of organic strategies, illuminating paths to a balanced, resilient garden ecosystem.

Cultural Controls: The First Line of Defense

The foundation of organic pest management lies in cultural controls, practices that naturally deter pests by creating an inhospitable environment for them.

- **Crop Rotation**: Rotating crops annually reduces the buildup of pests and diseases associated with specific plant families.
- **Companion Planting**: Growing certain plants together can repel pests or attract beneficial insects. For example, marigolds emit a scent that deters nematodes and tomato hornworms.
- **Sanitation**: Regularly removing plant debris and diseased plant material helps prevent the spread of pests and diseases.

Physical and Mechanical Controls: Barriers and Removal

When pests do make an appearance, physical and mechanical methods can be effective in keeping their numbers in check.

- **Hand Picking**: Simply removing pests by hand is often effective for larger invaders like Japanese beetles or tomato hornworms.
- **Barriers**: Floating row covers, netting, or collars made from cardboard can protect plants from pests ranging from cabbage moths to cutworms.
- **Water Sprays**: A strong jet of water can dislodge aphids, spider mites, and other small pests from plant foliage.

Biological Controls: Harnessing Nature's Predators

One of the most elegant organic solutions involves leveraging the garden's natural predator-prey relationships.

- **Beneficial Insects**: Ladybugs, lacewings, and predatory wasps are allies in the fight against aphids, caterpillars, and other pests. Planting flowers that attract these beneficial insects can help keep pest populations under control.
- **Nematodes**: Beneficial nematodes can be introduced to the soil to combat soil-dwelling pests like grub worms without harming plants or beneficial insects.
- **Bacillus thuringiensis (But)**: This naturally occurring bacterium can be applied to control caterpillar populations, as it is toxic only to them when ingested.

Organic Pesticides: Using With Care

When other methods are not enough, organic pesticides can be used as a last resort. These should be selected and applied carefully to minimize impact on beneficial insects and the environment.

- **Insecticidal Soap**: Effective against soft-bodied pests, insecticidal soaps must come into direct contact with the pest to be effective.
- **Neem Oil**: Derived from the neem tree, neem oil is a versatile pesticide that controls a wide range of pests and is safe for beneficial insects when used correctly.
- **Diatomaceous Earth**: Made from the fossilized remains of tiny aquatic organisms, diatomaceous earth can be sprinkled around plants to control slugs, snails, and other crawling pests.

Integrated Approaches: Combining Strategies for Maximum Effect

The most effective organic pest control strategy often involves combining several approaches to create a comprehensive defense.

- **Monitoring and Thresholds**: Regularly inspect plants for signs of pests and determine action thresholds – the point at which pest populations could cause significant damage and warrant intervention.
- **Timing and Precision**: Apply interventions at the most vulnerable stage of the pest's life cycle for maximum effectiveness, targeting treatments to affected areas to minimize impact on non-target species.

The Philosophy Behind Organic Pest Control

Organic pest control is more than a set of techniques; it's a philosophy that embraces the complexity of the garden ecosystem. It recognizes that pests are a natural part of the garden, seeking not to eliminate them but to manage their populations through balance and restraint. This approach fosters a deep respect for the interconnections within the garden, where every plant, pest, and predator play a role in the larger web of life.

The Impact of Organic Practices

By adopting organic pest control solutions, gardeners contribute to a larger movement towards sustainable living and ecological stewardship. These practices ensure that our gardens are safe havens for pollinators, beneficial insects, and wildlife, while also safeguarding the health of the soil and the broader environment. Furthermore, they remind us that our actions in the garden ripple outwards, affecting the delicate balance of our local ecosystems and, ultimately, the planet.

In conclusion, organic pest control is an integral part of cultivating a garden that is not only productive but also vibrant and life-sustaining. It challenges us to rethink our relationship with nature, encouraging a shift from dominance to partnership. Through the thoughtful application of these organic strategies, we nurture not just our gardens but also a deeper connection to the earth, laying the foundation for a more sustainable, resilient world.

PREVENTATIVE PRACTICES FOR DISEASE MANAGEMENT

In the garden, prevention is not just a practice but a philosophy, embracing foresight and stewardship to maintain the health and vitality of our plants. The essence of disease management lies not in combating diseases after they've taken hold, but in creating conditions that are inherently resistant to disease. This sub-chapter explores the preventative practices that form the cornerstone of disease management, guiding you through strategies to keep your garden thriving with minimal intervention.

Cultivating Healthy Soil

The foundation of a healthy garden is healthy soil. Rich, vibrant soil supports strong plant growth, which in itself can be the best defense against disease.

- **Organic Matter**: Regularly adding compost and other organic matter improves soil structure, water retention, and nutrient availability, creating an environment where plants can thrive.

- **Soil Testing and Balancing**: Periodic soil testing allows you to adjust pH levels and nutrient balances, tailoring your soil amendments to meet the specific needs of your garden.

Selecting Disease-Resistant Varieties

Plant breeding has given us a wealth of options when it comes to disease resistance. Choosing varieties that are naturally resistant to common diseases in your area can significantly reduce disease pressures.

- **Research and Selection**: Invest time in researching plant varieties before purchasing, looking for those labeled as disease-resistant.

- **Diversity**: Planting a diverse range of crops reduces the risk of widespread disease outbreaks, as different plants will be susceptible to different pathogens.

Ensuring Proper Spacing and Air Circulation

Plants need room to breathe. Proper spacing according to the specific needs of each plant ensures good air circulation, reducing the humidity that can foster fungal diseases.

- **Follow Planting Guides**: Adhere to recommended spacing guidelines, which are designed not just for the physical space plants need but also for optimal air flow.
- **Pruning**: Regularly pruning plants to remove dead or overlapping branches can improve air circulation and reduce disease incidence.

Watering Wisely

How, when, and how much you water can significantly impact your garden's disease resistance.

- **Water at the Base**: Avoid overhead watering, which can wet leaves and create ideal conditions for fungal diseases. Drip irrigation or soaker hoses target water directly to the root zone, where it's needed.
- **Morning Watering**: If overhead watering is necessary, do it in the morning to allow leaves to dry during the day.
- **Consistent Moisture**: Keeping the soil consistently moist (but not waterlogged) helps prevent plant stress, which can make plants more susceptible to disease.

Implementing Crop Rotation

Rotating crops annually can interrupt the lifecycle of soil-borne pathogens, reducing disease buildup over time.

- **Plan Your Rotation**: Avoid planting the same crop or crops from the same family in the same location for at least three years.
- **Record Keeping**: Maintain detailed records of what was planted where each year to aid in planning your crop rotation.

Encouraging Beneficial Microorganisms

The soil is alive with beneficial bacteria and fungi that can play a role in suppressing pathogenic organisms.

- **Compost Teas**: Applying aerated compost tea to your plants can introduce beneficial microorganisms to your plant's foliage and the soil, competing with and sometimes directly antagonizing disease-causing organisms.
- **Mycorrhizae**: Introducing mycorrhizal fungi to your soil can help form symbiotic relationships with plant roots, enhancing nutrient uptake and providing another layer of defense against certain soil pathogens.

Keeping the Garden Clean

Sanitation is a simple but often overlooked aspect of disease prevention.

- **Remove Diseased Plant Material**: Promptly remove and properly dispose of any diseased plant material. Do not compost diseased plants as this can spread pathogens.
- **Clean Tools and Containers**: Regularly disinfect gardening tools, pots, and trays used for planting to prevent the spread of disease from one part of the garden to another.

Using Mulches

Mulches can play a dual role in disease prevention by both retaining soil moisture and acting as a physical barrier between the soil and plant foliage.

- **Organic Mulches**: Wood chips, straw, or leaf mold can prevent soil-borne pathogens from splashing up onto lower plant leaves during rain or watering.
- **Reflective Mulches**: Certain metallic or synthetic mulches can deter pests that spread viral diseases and reduce the intensity of soil-borne diseases.

Monitoring and Early Intervention

Regular monitoring of your garden allows for the early detection of diseases, often enabling you to manage them before they become widespread.

- **Regular Inspections**: Make routine inspections of your garden a habit, looking out for signs of disease or stress in plants.
- **Isolation of New Plants**: Quarantine new plants before introducing them to your garden to ensure they are not carrying any diseases.

Embracing a Holistic Approach

Preventative practices for disease management in the garden are not just about avoiding disease; they're about cultivating a garden ecosystem that is balanced, resilient, and healthy. This holistic approach requires patience, observation, and a willingness to learn from the garden itself. It's a journey that goes beyond the mere absence of disease to embrace the flourishing of life in all its diversity.

By integrating these preventative practices into your gardening routine, you create not only a garden that is more resistant to disease but also a sanctuary that supports a rich tapestry of life. This approach to disease management is a reflection of a broader ethos of care, respect, and stewardship for the land, embodying the principles of sustainability and harmony with the natural world.

BENEFICIAL INSECTS AND HOW TO ATTRACT THEM

In the intricate dance of the garden ecosystem, beneficial insects play pivotal roles that go far beyond mere pollination. These natural allies, from the predatory ladybugs that feast on aphids to the parasitic wasps that lay their eggs in caterpillars, form the backbone of integrated pest and disease management. This sub-chapter delves into the fascinating world of beneficial insects, offering insights on how to attract these guardians to your garden, turning it into a stronghold of balance and health.

Understanding Beneficial Insects

Before we can invite these allies into our gardens, we must first understand who they are and the roles they play:

- **Predators**: Insects like ladybugs, lacewings, and ground beetles voraciously consume pests such as aphids, mites, and larvae, keeping their populations in check.
- **Parasitoids**: Parasitic wasps and certain types of flies lay their eggs on or in pest insects. Their larvae feed on the host, eventually controlling pest populations.
- **Pollinators**: While their primary role is in the pollination of plants, pollinators like bees and butterflies also contribute to the garden's health by ensuring plant reproduction and diversity.

Creating a Habitat for Beneficial Insects

Attracting beneficial insects is about creating a welcoming environment that meets their needs for food, water, and shelter.

- **Diverse Plantings**: A variety of plants, including annuals, perennials, herbs, and shrubs, can provide a year-round feast of nectar and pollen for beneficial insects. Flowers like dill, fennel, alyssum, and cosmos are particularly attractive to these insects.
- **Insectary Beds**: Dedicated areas planted specifically to attract beneficial insects can serve as insect sanctuaries, ensuring a steady population of natural pest controllers.
- **Leave Some Wild**: Allowing a part of your garden to grow a little wild can provide hiding spots and overwintering sites for beneficial insects. A pile of leaves or a deadwood stack can be a perfect habitat for predatory insects.

Supporting Beneficial Insects

Once beneficial insects have been attracted to your garden, it's crucial to support their survival and proliferation.

- **Avoid Chemical Pesticides**: Even organic or natural pesticides can harm beneficial insects. Use them only as a last resort and choose the least harmful options.
- **Provide Water**: A shallow dish filled with stones and water can offer a safe drinking spot for beneficial insects, ensuring they stay hydrated.
- **Timing Plantings**: Ensure that flowering plants are available throughout the growing season to provide continuous support for beneficial insect populations.

Recognizing Beneficial Insects

Learning to recognize beneficial insects is crucial to avoid mistakenly removing them from your garden.

- **Ladybugs**: Familiar and beloved, ladybugs are voracious predators of aphids and other soft-bodied pests.
- **Lacewings**: With their delicate, green wings, lacewings consume vast amounts of aphids, mites, and insect eggs.
- **Parasitic Wasps**: These tiny warriors are hard to notice but play a significant role in controlling pest populations without harming plants or other beneficial insects.

Encouraging a Balanced Ecosystem

The ultimate goal of attracting beneficial insects is to foster a balanced ecosystem where pests are managed naturally, without the need for intervention. This balance is the hallmark of a healthy garden, one that sustains itself with minimal human interference.

- **Observation**: Regularly observing your garden not only helps you spot pest problems early but also allows you to witness the beneficial interactions that take place, giving you insights into the health of your garden's ecosystem.
- **Patience**: Establishing a balanced ecosystem takes time. It requires patience and the understanding that occasional pest outbreaks are part of the natural cycle and can actually serve to attract more beneficial insects to your garden.

The Broader Impact

Attracting beneficial insects to your garden does more than just enhance your own little patch of green; it contributes to the health of the wider ecosystem. By providing a refuge for these insects, you're supporting biodiversity, bolstering local populations of beneficial insects that can aid in the balance of natural areas beyond your garden.

Cultivating Coexistence

Embracing beneficial insects in the garden teaches us about coexistence and the value of each creature in the web of life. It's a practice that aligns with the principles of organic gardening and sustainability, where every action is taken with mindfulness of its impact on the broader ecosystem. In this way, the garden becomes not just a place of cultivation but a sanctuary for life in all its forms.

Through the strategic attraction and support of beneficial insects, gardeners can harness the power of nature to maintain the health and vitality of their gardens. This approach is a testament to the wisdom of working with nature rather than against it, fostering a garden that is not only productive but also a vibrant, living ecosystem. As we learn to recognize and support these insect allies, we take an active role in the stewardship of our environment, cultivating gardens that are a testament to the beauty and balance of nature.

CONCLUSION

As we conclude our journey through the intricate landscape of **Integrated Pest and Disease Management**, we stand equipped not just with strategies and techniques but with a profound appreciation for the balance and harmony within our gardens. This chapter has guided us through the delicate dance of nurturing our plants while coexisting with the myriad of other life forms that inhabit our garden spaces. It's here we've learned that managing pests and diseases is not about waging war but about fostering an environment where balance and health are the cornerstones of garden vitality.

The Philosophy of Coexistence

Our exploration has underscored a philosophy of coexistence, emphasizing preventative measures, cultural practices, and natural remedies that align with the cycles of nature. This approach has not only shown us how to minimize the impact of pests and diseases but has also illuminated the ways in which these challenges can become opportunities for growth, learning, and greater ecological understanding.

The Art of Observation

Key to our journey has been the art of observation—a skill that allows us to detect imbalances early and respond with precision and thoughtfulness. This vigilant watchfulness is our first line of defense, enabling us to act swiftly and effectively, often preventing minor issues from escalating into major problems. Through observation, we've learned to read the signs of our garden, becoming attuned to its needs and rhythms.

Building Resilience

Building resilience within our garden ecosystem has emerged as a central theme, highlighting the importance of diversity, soil health, and the cultivation of strong, vigorous plants. These practices, integral to integrated pest and disease management, ensure our gardens are not just surviving but thriving, capable of withstanding the inevitable challenges that come their way.

Embracing Natural Allies

We've also discovered the value of embracing our natural allies, from beneficial insects to microbial friends in the soil, each playing a critical role in the garden's defense system. By supporting these natural protectors, we enhance our garden's ability to self-regulate, reducing the need for intervention and allowing nature to guide the way toward health and balance.

A Journey Forward

In closing, **Integrated Pest and Disease Management** has been more than a manual; it has been a journey toward understanding and implementing practices that respect and reflect the complexities of the natural world. As we move forward, let us carry these lessons into our gardens and beyond, cultivating spaces that are not only productive but also vibrant reflections of the ecological balance we strive to achieve. Here's to the gardens we tend, the knowledge we've gained, and the future we're shaping—one plant, one garden, at a time.

BOOK 7: SPECIALIZED GARDENING TECHNIQUES

As we draw the curtain on our deep dive into **Specialized Gardening Techniques**, it's clear that the journey through this chapter has been one of exploration, innovation, and adaptation. We've navigated the intricate landscapes of raised bed gardening, embraced the challenges and rewards of container and urban gardening, delved into the future-forward practices of hydroponics and aquaponics, and scaled the vertical heights of gardening in small spaces. Each section has not only expanded our toolkit but also broadened our perspective on what it means to cultivate life in the most diverse and sometimes challenging environments.

The Essence of Adaptation

This chapter has underscored a fundamental truth: gardening is an act of adaptation. It's about meeting nature halfway, using ingenuity and creativity to overcome spatial, environmental, and resource limitations. Raised bed gardening has taught us how to create fertile oases in areas where the ground is hard, rocky, or otherwise unsuitable for traditional gardening. Container and urban gardening have revealed the possibilities for bringing nature into the densest of urban environments, turning balconies, rooftops, and even windowsills into verdant havens.

The Innovation of Hydroponics and Aquaponics

Venturing into the realms of hydroponics and aquaponics, we've glimpsed the future of gardening—an efficient, soil-less cultivation of plants that conserves water and space while potentially yielding more abundant harvests. These methods embody the cutting edge of gardening technology, where the symbiosis between fish and plants in aquaponics or the precision nutrient delivery in hydroponics can create self-sustaining ecosystems. This exploration has not just been about learning new techniques; it's been about reimagining the possibilities of what our gardens can be.

The Artistry of Vertical Gardening

Vertical gardening has taught us to look up and see the sky, not as the limit, but as a new frontier. This technique has opened up a world of possibilities for those with limited space, allowing us to grow upwards and make the most of every square inch of our urban environments. It's a testament to the gardener's creativity, proving that limitations can indeed be the mother of invention.

A Celebration of Diversity and Resilience

Throughout this journey, we've celebrated the diversity of gardening methods and the resilience of gardeners in the face of challenges. These specialized techniques are not just about growing plants; they're about growing communities, fostering sustainability, and nurturing well-being. They encourage us to think outside the box—or, in this case, the garden bed—inspiring us to apply these principles not only in our gardening practices but in our lives.

Looking Forward

As we conclude this chapter, let us carry forward the spirit of innovation and adaptation that has permeated these pages. The world of gardening is ever-evolving, and so too are the challenges we face—from changing climates to urbanization. The techniques we've explored here equip us not just to navigate these challenges but to thrive amidst them, creating lush, productive gardens in spaces we once thought impossible.

A Call to Action

This is not merely the end of a chapter but a call to action—a prompt to experiment with these specialized gardening techniques in our own spaces, whether that's a small apartment balcony, a rooftop, or a backyard. Let's approach these practices with curiosity and creativity, remembering that each plant we nurture is a step toward a greener, more sustainable world.

The Garden as a Reflection of the Gardener

Ultimately, our gardens are reflections of us—their diversity, resilience, and beauty mirror our own. As we venture forward, experimenting with raised beds, containers, hydroponics, aquaponics, and vertical gardens, let's view each success and setback as a part of the journey, a learning experience that deepens our connection to the earth and to each other.

In the spirit of **Specialized Gardening Techniques**, let's embrace the challenges, celebrate the victories, and continue to grow—not just our gardens but our communities and ourselves. Here's to the endless possibilities that await us in our gardens, to the innovations on the horizon, and to the joy of cultivating life, no matter where we are. Let's keep planting, growing, and thriving, for in every seed lies the promise of a new beginning, and in every gardener, the heart of a pioneer,

Leroy Karper

In the vibrant tapestry of gardening, where tradition weaves through the fabric of innovation, lies the heart of **Specialized Gardening Techniques**. This chapter is an odyssey into the realms of creativity and adaptation, exploring the fertile edges where conventional gardening meets the ingenuity required to flourish under unique conditions. It's here, in the dance between the gardener's vision and the garden's potential, that we discover the myriad ways to cultivate life beyond the bounds of traditional plots.

Gardening, at its essence, is an act of partnership with the earth, a collaboration that nurtures not just plants but the soul of the gardener. Yet, not all gardens are born from wide, open spaces basking in uninterrupted sunlight. Many thrive on balconies high above city streets, in small patches of soil surrounded by concrete, or even in the controlled environments of indoor spaces. It's within these unconventional spaces that gardening techniques must evolve, transforming limitations into opportunities for growth and innovation.

Raised Bed Gardening: A New Perspective

Venturing into raised bed gardening, we elevate our sights and our soils, creating lush, productive gardens in spaces where traditional gardening might falter. Raised beds offer a canvas for creativity, allowing gardeners to control soil composition, improve drainage, and tailor their gardening efforts to meet the specific needs of their plants. This section will guide you through designing, building, and cultivating raised beds, turning even the most challenging spaces into bountiful oases.

Container and Urban Gardening: Thriving in Limited Spaces

The heart of the city, with its hustle and limited space, might seem an unlikely setting for a garden, yet it's here that container and urban gardening shine. These techniques redefine what it means to garden, proving that even the smallest balcony or windowsill can become a haven for growth. We'll explore how to select containers, choose plants suited for urban life, and maximize your space for productivity and beauty, crafting urban evens that bring nature to your doorstep.

Hydroponics and Aquaponics: The Future of Gardening

In the realms of hydroponics and aquaponics, we step into the future of gardening— a world where soil is optional, and plants grow in nutrient-rich water, sometimes in symbiosis with fish. These systems offer a sustainable, efficient approach to gardening, ideal for indoor environments and areas with poor soil quality. This section will dive into the basics of setting up your system, understanding the science behind the growth, and harvesting the fruits (and vegetables) of your labor in these soil-less gardens.

Vertical Gardening: Growing Upwards

When horizontal space is at a premium, we turn our gazes upward. Vertical gardening is an art form that maximizes the vertical planes in our homes and gardens, creating living walls of foliage and flowers. This technique not only expands our gardening space but also transforms our living environments, bringing lush, green vitality to the most unexpected places. Here, we'll explore the structures and plants best suited for vertical gardening, offering inspiration and guidance for elevating your gardening aspirations.

The Journey Beyond Traditional Boundaries

Specialized Gardening Techniques is more than a compilation of methods; it's a journey beyond the traditional boundaries of gardening. It's a testament to the gardener's resilience, creativity, and unyielding passion for cultivating life in all its forms. These techniques are not just about overcoming limitations; they're about reimagining what a garden can be, pushing the envelope of possibility to create spaces that reflect the diversity and adaptability of nature itself.

As we delve into this chapter, let us do so with open minds and adventurous spirits, ready to embrace the unconventional and explore the frontiers of gardening. Whether you're crafting a raised bed out of reclaimed wood, potting herbs for your kitchen windowsill, setting up a hydroponic system in your basement, or weaving a tapestry of greenery up a trellis, remember that each act of gardening is a step towards a greener, more vibrant world.

In the pages that follow, let the limitations of space and soil inspire rather than inhibit, as we uncover the boundless potential of gardens crafted with care, imagination, and a deep love for the earth. Welcome to **Specialized Gardening Techniques**, where every gardener finds a way to let their garden grow, no matter the obstacles. Let's embark on this adventure together, cultivating not just plants but possibilities, as we grow our gardens and ourselves in harmony with the ever-expansive canvas of gardening.

RAISED BED GARDENING

Raised bed gardening is a testament to the gardener's innovation, a method that transcends the limitations of traditional in-ground gardening by elevating the cultivation space. This specialized technique offers an array of benefits, from improved soil conditions and drainage to enhanced ergonomics and aesthetic appeal. Let's delve into the essence of raised bed gardening, exploring how to design, create, and nurture these elevated sanctuaries of growth.

The Foundation of Raised Bed Gardening

At its core, raised bed gardening involves the creation of contained soil areas elevated above the natural ground level. These beds can be constructed from a variety of materials, including wood, stone, bricks, or even recycled plastics, forming a versatile solution for diverse garden settings.

- **Design Considerations**: When designing a raised bed, consider factors such as orientation for optimal sunlight, accessibility for maintenance, and the integration of irrigation systems. The dimensions of the bed should allow easy reach to the center from all sides, typically no wider than four feet.

Advantages of Raised Bed Gardening

Raised beds provide distinct advantages that can transform the gardening experience:

- **Enhanced Soil Control**: Filling beds with a custom soil mix allows for perfect tailoring to plant needs, bypassing the challenges of native soil conditions.

- **Improved Drainage**: The elevated design promotes efficient drainage, crucial for healthy root development.
- **Extended Growing Season**: Soil in raised beds warms up more quickly in spring, offering an earlier start to the growing season.
- **Reduced Strain**: The height of raised beds minimizes bending and stooping, making gardening more accessible and enjoyable.
- **Pest and Weed Management**: Raised beds can simplify the control of weeds and deter some ground-dwelling pests.

Building Your Raised Bed

Creating a raised bed is an invitation to blend functionality with creativity:

- **Materials**: Choose materials that are durable and non-toxic. Untreated cedar or redwood offers natural rot resistance, while stone or brick can provide a more permanent structure.
- **Construction**: Ensure the bed is level and securely assembled. For wood constructions, consider using corner posts for added stability. Drainage can be enhanced by laying a gravel base or perforated landscape fabric at the bottom.

Soil and Planting

The soul of the raised bed is its soil—a blend chosen by the gardener to nourish and sustain:

- **Soil Mix**: A mix of topsoil, compost, and other amendments like perlite or vermiculite can create a fertile, well-draining growing medium.
- **Planting Strategy**: Raised beds offer the opportunity for intensive planting, maximizing space through strategies like square foot gardening or intercropping.

Maintenance and Care

Caring for a raised bed garden involves ongoing attention to ensure its vitality:

- **Watering**: While raised beds promote drainage, they can also dry out faster. Drip irrigation or soaker hoses can provide consistent, efficient moisture.
- **Mulching**: Applying a layer of organic mulch helps retain soil moisture, suppress weeds, and gradually enrich the soil.
- **Seasonal Refresh**: Replenishing the soil with compost or other organic matter each season keeps the bed productive year after year.

Troubleshooting Common Challenges

Even with their many benefits, raised beds can encounter specific challenges:

- **Soil Settlement**: Over time, soil in raised beds may settle or compact. Regularly loosening the soil and adding fresh amendments can maintain its structure.
- **Wooden Bed Maintenance**: Wood frames will eventually weather and decay. Inspecting and replacing damaged boards as needed ensures the longevity of the bed.

Expanding the Raised Bed Garden

As confidence and experience grow, so too can your raised bed garden. Additional beds can be added over time, creating a tapestry of productivity that caters to a wide array of crops. Consider incorporating vertical elements like trellises or arches for climbing plants, adding both functionality and visual interest.

The Raised Bed Community

Beyond the confines of the individual garden, raised bed gardening fosters a sense of community. Sharing designs, experiences, and harvests with fellow gardeners can inspire and enrich the collective gardening journey. Community gardens often utilize raised beds to manage space efficiently, bringing together people of diverse backgrounds to grow food and flowers in shared harmony.

The Sustainability of Raised Beds

In the broader context of sustainable gardening, raised beds represent a method that can reduce water usage, minimize soil disturbance, and encourage organic practices. By concentrating resources and care into a defined area, gardeners can achieve remarkable productivity with minimal environmental impact.

Embracing the Raised Bed

Raised bed gardening is not just a method; it's a reflection of the gardener's adaptability and creativity. It demonstrates that, with thoughtfulness and care, we can create environments where plants thrive, regardless of the ground beneath them. These elevated plots are more than just containers for soil; they are vessels of possibility, where the seeds of today's efforts bloom into the abundant harvests of tomorrow.

In embracing raised bed gardening, we commit ourselves to a practice that is both ancient and innovative, blending the wisdom of the past with the possibilities of the future. It's a testament to the enduring human connection to the earth, a reminder that, no matter the challenges we face, we can always find a way to cultivate beauty, nourishment, and life.

CONTAINER AND URBAN GARDENING

In the heart of the city's concrete expanse, where the green is sparse and the soil scarce, container and urban gardening emerge as beacons of verdant hope. This specialized gardening technique transforms balconies, rooftops, and even the smallest of spaces into lush, productive oases, challenging the notion that one needs vast expanses of land to cultivate beauty and sustenance. Let's journey through the principles of container and urban gardening, discovering how to bring the bounty of the earth into the urban environment.

The Essence of Container Gardening

Container gardening is the art of growing plants in pots or other receptacles instead of planting them in the ground. It's a practice that embodies flexibility and creativity, allowing gardeners to cultivate a wide array of plants, from ornamental flowers to a full array of vegetables and herbs, regardless of their ground soil's quality or availability.

- **Container Choices**: From traditional clay pots to inventive repurposed objects, the choice of container can add personality to your urban garden. Ensure each container has adequate drainage to prevent root rot.
- **Soil and Fertilization**: Use high-quality potting mix designed for container gardening, enriched with compost or a balanced, slow-release organic fertilizer to nourish your plants.

Maximizing Limited Spaces

Urban gardening thrives on making the most of limited spaces. Balconies, windowsills, and rooftops can be transformed into vibrant gardens with a bit of ingenuity.

- **Vertical Gardening**: Utilize vertical space by installing trellises, shelves, or hanging baskets. Climbing plants like tomatoes, peas, and certain flowers can flourish upwards, offering both beauty and yield.
- **Succession Planting**: Rotate crops in your containers to ensure a continuous harvest. After harvesting one plant, replace it with another, considering the changing light and temperature conditions through the seasons.

Watering Wisdom in Container Gardening

Water management is crucial in container gardening, as pots can dry out faster than ground soil, especially in the heat of summer.

- **Consistent Monitoring**: Check the moisture level of your containers daily, as the need for water can change rapidly with weather conditions.
- **Self-Watering Containers**: Consider using or making self-watering containers, which include a reservoir at the bottom, reducing the frequency of watering and ensuring plants have consistent access to moisture.

Urban Gardening Beyond the Balcony

Urban gardening extends beyond individual containers, embracing community spaces and shared initiatives.

- **Community Gardens**: Participating in or starting a community garden can offer not just space to grow but also a sense of connection and collective resilience.
- **Green Roofs and Walls**: Transforming rooftops and walls into green spaces can not only provide gardening opportunities but also contribute to urban biodiversity and help regulate building temperatures.

Pollinators in the City

Attracting pollinators is as crucial in urban settings as it is in rural gardens. Even in the heart of the city, gardens can become havens for bees, butterflies, and other beneficial insects.

- **Pollinator-Friendly Plants**: Incorporate plants known to attract pollinators, such as lavender, borage, and marigolds, ensuring that your urban garden contributes to the health of the local ecosystem.

The Challenge of Urban Pests

Urban gardens may face unique pest challenges, from pigeons and squirrels to the more familiar aphids and slugs.

- **Natural Deterrents**: Employ natural deterrents and barriers to protect your plants. For example, netting can safeguard against birds, while companion planting with strong-scented herbs may repel insect pests.

Sustainable Urban Gardening Practices

Sustainability is a cornerstone of urban gardening, reflecting a commitment to environmentally responsible practices.

- **Organic Methods**: Opt for organic pest control and fertilization methods to minimize environmental impact.
- **Water Conservation**: Collect rainwater for irrigation, and choose drought-resistant plant varieties to reduce water usage.

Community and Well-being

Urban gardening fosters community bonds and personal well-being, creating pockets of tranquility and connection in the urban landscape.

- **Shared Spaces, Shared Lives**: Gardens can become communal spaces for sharing knowledge, produce, and moments of beauty, enriching the urban experience.
- **Mental Health Benefits**: Engaging with plants and soil has been shown to reduce stress and improve mood, offering a counterbalance to the hustle of city life.

Embracing the Urban Canvas

Container and urban gardening invite us to reimagine the possibilities of city living, proving that even in the most unlikely spaces, growth and abundance can flourish. These gardens are not just retreats from the urban environment but vibrant expressions of resilience, creativity, and the enduring human impulse to connect with nature.

In cultivating these urban oases, we not only enhance our immediate surroundings but also contribute to a larger movement toward sustainable, inclusive urban ecosystems. Through the simple act of planting in containers, we join a community of urban gardeners worldwide, transforming balconies and rooftops into links in a global chain of green spaces, each a testament to the power of growth against the odds.

Container and urban gardening embody a profound act of hope and defiance, a declaration that even in the heart of the concrete jungle, life—in all its green, thriving glory—can find a way.

HYDROPONICS AND AQUAPONICS BASICS

Venturing into the realms of hydroponics and aquaponics opens gardeners to innovative worlds where water becomes the nurturing medium for plant life. These techniques, remarkable in their efficiency and sustainability, offer a futuristic yet profoundly natural way of cultivating plants. Here, we explore the basics of hydroponics and aquaponics, guiding you through the principles that make these systems a cornerstone of modern gardening practices.

Hydroponics: Gardening Without Soil

At its core, hydroponics is the science of growing plants in nutrient-rich water instead of soil. This technique harnesses water's natural roles as both carrier and solvent to deliver nutrients directly to plant roots, facilitating a more efficient uptake than traditional soil-based cultivation.

- **The Basics**: Hydroponic systems can vary from simple, passive setups to complex, automated systems. Common types include the nutrient film technique (NFT), deep water culture (DWC), and ebb and flow systems. Each system has its unique mechanics, but all share the principle of exposing plant roots to a nutrient solution while providing adequate oxygenation to foster growth.

- **Advantages**: Hydroponics allows for precise control over nutrient levels, eliminates soil-borne diseases, and often results in higher yields and faster growth rates. It's an ideal solution for space-limited environments, including urban settings and indoor gardens.

- **Challenges**: Maintaining the right nutrient balance, pH levels, and oxygenation requires careful monitoring and adjustment. Initial setup costs can be higher compared to traditional gardening, but the efficiency and productivity of hydroponic systems often justify the investment.

Aquaponics: A Symbiotic Ecosystem

Aquaponics combines hydroponics with aquaculture (raising fish) in a closed-loop system that mimics natural ecosystems. Here, the waste produced by fish enriches the water with nutrients, which are then absorbed by plants, purifying the water in return.

- **The Cycle**: Fish release ammonia into the water, which beneficial bacteria convert into nitrates—a key nutrient for plant growth. Plants, in turn, filter and clean the water, which is recirculated back to the fish. This symbiotic relationship creates a self-sustaining environment where both fish and plants can thrive.

- **System Components**: A basic aquaponics setup includes a fish tank, a grow bed for the plants, and a pump to circulate water between the two. Media beds filled with porous materials like clay pebbles, or floating rafts, can support plant roots and facilitate filtration.

- **Benefits**: Aquaponics is a water-efficient, organic method that produces both fresh produce and protein (fish) without the need for chemical fertilizers. It's particularly suited for areas with poor soil quality or water scarcity.

- **Considerations**: Balancing the needs of both fish and plants requires attention to system design and water quality management. The choice of fish species (tilapia, goldfish, or koi are popular options) and plants must be compatible in terms of temperature and pH preferences.

Setting Up Your System

Whether you choose hydroponics or aquaponics, starting with a simple, manageable system is key. Research thoroughly and consider starting with a kit that includes all necessary components. As you gain experience, you can expand or customize your system to fit your needs.

- **Learning and Patience**: Understanding the dynamics of nutrient solutions, plant needs, and fish health takes time. Regular testing of water parameters and careful observation will guide your adjustments and interventions.
- **Community and Resources**: Engage with the hydroponic and aquaponic gardening communities, both online and in person. Workshops, forums, and clubs can provide invaluable advice, troubleshooting tips, and inspiration.

The Future of Gardening

Hydroponics and aquaponics represent more than just alternative gardening methods—they embody a shift towards more sustainable, efficient, and innovative approaches to food production. In the face of environmental challenges, urbanization, and the growing need for sustainable agricultural practices, these systems offer a glimpse into the future of gardening and farming.

- **Sustainability**: By dramatically reducing water usage, eliminating the need for soil, and enabling local food production, hydroponics and aquaponics contribute to a more sustainable world.
- **Empowerment**: These systems democratize gardening, making it accessible to everyone, regardless of land availability or soil quality. They empower urban dwellers, educators, and commercial growers alike to produce fresh, healthy food in a fraction of the space required by traditional farming.

Embracing Water as the Source of Life

Hydroponics and aquaponics teach us to see water not just as a necessity for plant growth, but as the very medium through which life can flourish. These systems challenge us to think creatively about space, resources, and our relationship with food. They encourage us to envision gardens not as bound to the earth, but as vibrant ecosystems where water, plants, and fish coexist in harmony.

As we explore these specialized gardening techniques, we're reminded of the adaptability of nature and the potential for innovation to align with ecological principles. Hydroponics and aquaponics are not just about growing plants and fish; they're about cultivating a future where sustainability, efficiency, and abundance go hand in hand. In embracing these methods, we step into a world of gardening that is as boundless as the water cycle itself, a cycle that sustains all life on our planet.

VERTICAL GARDENING FOR SMALL SPACES

Vertical gardening is a transformative approach that turns the concept of gardening on its side—literally. It's an ingenious solution to the challenge of limited space, making it possible to grow lush, productive gardens in the smallest of footprints. By reaching upwards, vertical gardening exploits untapped aerial space, allowing urban dwellers, apartment residents, and those with more ambition than land to cultivate an array of plants. This sub-chapter explores the principles, practices, and profound potential of vertical gardening.

The Essence of Vertical Gardening

Vertical gardening is the practice of growing plants upward using trellises, walls, towers, or hanging containers, rather than spreading them out across the ground. This method is not just about saving space; it's about reimagining the possibilities of gardening environments.

Benefits of Going Vertical

- **Space Efficiency**: Vertical gardens use minimal ground space, making them ideal for balconies, patios, and urban yards.
- **Accessibility**: Elevated gardens are easier to tend, reducing the need for bending and stooping, making gardening more accessible to everyone.
- **Microclimate Control**: Vertical gardens can create beneficial microclimates, providing shade or wind protection to sensitive plants.
- **Aesthetic Appeal**: Beyond their practical benefits, vertical gardens add visual interest and beauty to any space, transforming bland walls and fences into living art.

Designing Your Vertical Garden

- **Choosing a Structure**: Options range from simple trellises and supports for climbing plants to elaborate vertical planting systems with built-in irrigation. Consider your space, the plants you wish to grow, and your budget when selecting a structure.
- **Selecting Plants**: Some plants are naturally suited to vertical growth, including vining vegetables (like cucumbers and beans), climbing flowers (such

as clematis and morning glories), and sprawling herbs (like thyme and oregano). Even non-climbing plants can be adapted to vertical gardening with the right support.

- **Light and Exposure**: Assess the light exposure of your vertical garden's location. Ensure that the arrangement of plants takes into consideration their light requirements, with taller plants not overshadowing shorter ones that need full sun.

Constructing Vertical Gardens

- **DIY Projects**: Many vertical gardens can be created with basic materials and a little ingenuity. Pallet gardens, ladder shelves, and hanging pocket gardens are all accessible projects for the DIY enthusiast.
- **Professional Systems**: For those seeking more sophisticated solutions, professional vertical gardening systems offer integrated watering and nutrient delivery mechanisms, designed for maximum productivity and ease of use.

Maintenance and Care

- **Watering**: Vertical gardens may require more frequent watering than traditional gardens due to increased exposure and drainage. Drip irrigation systems can be particularly effective for ensuring consistent moisture without overwatering.
- **Nutrition**: Regular feeding with liquid fertilizers ensures that vertical garden plants receive the nutrients they need, given the limited soil volume they often have.
- **Pruning and Training**: Regular pruning and training help manage growth and maintain the health and appearance of vertical gardens. Use ties and supports to guide plants as they grow.

Challenges and Solutions

- **Weight Considerations**: Ensure that structures are securely anchored and capable of supporting the weight of soil, plants, and water. Safety should always be a priority.
- **Pest Management**: Vertical gardens can still be susceptible to pests and diseases. Monitor plants regularly and adopt integrated pest management practices to address any issues promptly.

Expanding the Vertical Concept

- **Edible Walls**: Create a living pantry with vertical gardens dedicated to herbs, leafy greens, and small vegetables. Not only do they provide fresh produce, but they also bring vibrancy and life to cooking spaces, balconies, and outdoor areas.

- **Succulent Walls**: Succulents are particularly well-suited to vertical gardening, requiring minimal water and care. Their varied textures and colors can create stunning living tapestries.

- **Pollinator Attractors**: Incorporating flowering plants into vertical gardens can attract pollinators, adding another layer of life and activity to your garden space.

Vertical Gardening: A Symbol of Innovation

Vertical gardening represents more than a solution to spatial constraints; it symbolizes a broader movement towards innovative, sustainable urban living. It challenges us to think creatively about our environments, to see potential where we might have seen limitation, and to cultivate beauty and productivity in every available space.

Through vertical gardening, we're reminded that the essence of gardening isn't bound by traditional horizons. It's a dynamic interplay between humans and nature, an expression of care that reaches upwards, inviting us to grow gardens that not only nourish the body but also uplift the spirit. In embracing vertical gardening, we embrace a future where gardens are not just possible in every space but are celebrated as essential elements of urban life, bringing greenery, vibrancy, and biodiversity to the heart of our cities.

CONCLUSION

As we draw the curtain on our deep dive into **Specialized Gardening Techniques**, it's clear that the journey through this chapter has been one of exploration, innovation, and adaptation. We've navigated the intricate landscapes of raised bed gardening, embraced the challenges and rewards of container and urban gardening, delved into the future-forward practices of hydroponics and aquaponics, and scaled the vertical heights of gardening in small spaces. Each section has not only expanded our toolkit but also broadened our perspective on what it means to cultivate life in the most diverse and sometimes challenging environments.

The Essence of Adaptation

This chapter has underscored a fundamental truth: gardening is an act of adaptation. It's about meeting nature halfway, using ingenuity and creativity to overcome spatial, environmental, and resource limitations. Raised bed gardening has taught us how to create fertile oases in areas where the ground is hard, rocky, or otherwise unsuitable for traditional gardening. Container and urban gardening have revealed the possibilities for bringing nature into the densest of urban environments, turning balconies, rooftops, and even windowsills into verdant havens.

The Innovation of Hydroponics and Aquaponics

Venturing into the realms of hydroponics and aquaponics, we've glimpsed the future of gardening—an efficient, soil-less cultivation of plants that conserves water and space while potentially yielding more abundant harvests. These methods embody the cutting edge of gardening technology, where the symbiosis between fish and plants in aquaponics or the precision nutrient delivery in hydroponics can create self-sustaining ecosystems. This exploration has not just been about learning new techniques; it's been about reimagining the possibilities of what our gardens can be.

The Artistry of Vertical Gardening

Vertical gardening has taught us to look up and see the sky, not as the limit, but as a new frontier. This technique has opened up a world of possibilities for those with limited space, allowing us to grow upwards and make the most of every square inch of our urban environments. It's a testament to the gardener's creativity, proving that limitations can indeed be the mother of invention.

A Celebration of Diversity and Resilience

Throughout this journey, we've celebrated the diversity of gardening methods and the resilience of gardeners in the face of challenges. These specialized techniques are not just about growing plants; they're about growing communities, fostering sustainability, and nurturing well-being. They encourage us to think outside the box—or, in this case, the garden bed—inspiring us to apply these principles not only in our gardening practices but in our lives.

Looking Forward

As we conclude this chapter, let us carry forward the spirit of innovation and adaptation that has permeated these pages. The world of gardening is ever-evolving, and so too are the challenges we face—from changing climates to urbanization. The techniques we've explored here equip us not just to navigate these challenges but to thrive amidst them, creating lush, productive gardens in spaces we once thought impossible.

A Call to Action

This is not merely the end of a chapter but a call to action—a prompt to experiment with these specialized gardening techniques in our own spaces, whether that's a small apartment balcony, a rooftop, or a backyard. Let's approach these practices with curiosity and creativity, remembering that each plant we nurture is a step toward a greener, more sustainable world.

The Garden as a Reflection of the Gardener

Ultimately, our gardens are reflections of us—their diversity, resilience, and beauty mirror our own. As we venture forward, experimenting with raised beds, containers, hydroponics, aquaponics, and vertical gardens, let's view each success and setback as a part of the journey, a learning experience that deepens our connection to the earth and to each other.

In the spirit of **Specialized Gardening Techniques**, let's embrace the challenges, celebrate the victories, and continue to grow—not just our gardens but our communities and ourselves. Here's to the endless possibilities that await us in our gardens, to the innovations on the horizon, and to the joy of cultivating life, no matter where we are. Let's keep planting, growing, and thriving, for in every seed lies the promise of a new beginning, and in every gardener, the heart of a pioneer, ready to explore the uncharted territories of the natural world.

BOOK 8: HARVESTING, STORING, AND PRESERVING

At the heart of every garden lies the promise of harvest—a time when the fruits of diligent planning, planting, and care come to fruition. But the journey doesn't end with the plucking of a ripe tomato or the cutting of fragrant herbs; it extends into the thoughtful storing and preserving of our bounty, ensuring that the abundance of the growing season enriches our meals and lives throughout the year. This chapter unfolds the art and science of **Harvesting, Storing, and Preserving**, a trio of practices that are as ancient as agriculture itself, yet continually evolving to embrace new knowledge and techniques.

Harvesting is the gardener's final act of collaboration with nature, requiring patience, knowledge, and a keen eye to determine the precise moment when vegetables, fruits, and herbs have reached their peak. This section will guide you through the signs of readiness, the tools of the trade, and the methods that ensure the integrity of your harvest, capturing the essence of each season.

Transitioning to **Storing**, we navigate the challenge of extending the life of our harvest. Beyond mere longevity, proper storage techniques preserve the nutritional value, flavor, and texture of our produce. From root cellars to modern refrigerators, from airy baskets to sealed containers, this segment offers strategies for maintaining the freshness and vitality of each harvest, whether for weeks or months.

Preserving then becomes an act of transformation, where creativity meets sustainability. It's where the vibrant flavors of summer can be bottled, dried, frozen, or fermented to enhance winter meals. This section delves into the varied methods of preserving—canning, drying, freezing, fermenting, and more—each with its own history, technique, and joy. Preserving is not just about saving food; it's about enriching our culinary traditions, exploring new flavors, and celebrating the garden's generosity.

Together, **Harvesting, Storing, and Preserving** represent a full circle, from seed to sustenance, emphasizing not just the cyclical nature of gardening but its role in sustaining and enhancing our lives. This chapter is a tribute to the bounty of the earth and the ingenuity of those who cultivate and cherish it. As we explore these practices, we do more than just extend the life of our harvest; we weave the essence of the garden into the fabric of our daily lives, ensuring that its gifts are enjoyed to the fullest, shared widely, and remembered fondly, long after the seasons change.

SIGNS OF RIPENESS AND HARVESTING TECHNIQUES

Harvesting is the grand crescendo of the gardening season, a time of anticipation and reward, where each fruit, vegetable, and herb offers its bounty in turn. Recognizing the signs of ripeness and mastering harvesting techniques are crucial skills for every gardener, ensuring that produce is picked at its peak for the best flavor, nutrition, and storage longevity. This sub-chapter explores the art of identifying ripeness and the various techniques suited to harvesting a diverse garden.

Understanding Ripeness

Ripeness is not merely a moment but a symphony of signs and signals that vary widely across different types of produce.

- **Color**: Often the most visible indicator, a change in color can signify ripeness, such as tomatoes turning a deep red or green peppers taking on a vibrant yellow or red hue.
- **Texture**: Many fruits soften as they ripen. A gentle squeeze can indicate readiness, especially for fruits like peaches and avocados.
- **Aroma**: Ripening often releases aromatic compounds. A sniff test near the stem end can reveal if fruits like melons and strawberries are ready to harvest.
- **Taste**: Sometimes, the true test of ripeness is taste. Sampling a small piece can be the deciding factor for many vegetables and fruits.
- **Size**: While size can indicate maturity, it's important to know the expected size for each variety, as some are naturally smaller or larger when ripe.

Harvesting Techniques by Plant Type

Leafy Greens: Harvest in the cool of the morning when leaves are most turgid. For cut-and-come-again varieties, pick outer leaves only, allowing the center to continue growing.

Root Vegetables: Check for size by gently uncovering the top of the root. Harvest by loosening the soil around the plant with a fork before gently pulling it out.

Fruiting Vegetables: Use a sharp knife or scissors to cut fruits from the plant, leaving a small piece of stem attached. This technique reduces damage to the plant and the fruit.

Berries: Harvest gently with a twisting motion to avoid crushing. Berries should be fully colored and come off the stem easily if ripe.

Tree Fruits: Look for a slight give when pressed gently near the stem. Many tree fruits will also detach easily with a gentle upward twist when ripe.

Special Considerations for Harvesting

- **Morning Harvest**: Whenever possible, harvest in the early morning when the plant's water content is highest. This ensures the crispest texture and longest shelf life.
- **Tool Care**: Keep harvesting tools clean and sharp. This minimizes damage and potential disease transmission between plants.
- **Handling Care**: Handle all produce gently to avoid bruising, which can accelerate spoilage. Use baskets or containers that allow air circulation and avoid overloading.

Post-Harvest Handling

Immediately after harvesting, proper handling is key to maintaining quality.

- **Cooling**: Some produce, especially leafy greens and root vegetables, benefits from being cooled quickly after harvest to retain freshness.
- **Cleaning**: Gently clean soil and debris from vegetables and fruits. However, delay washing until right before use to prevent moisture-related spoilage.
- **Curing**: Certain vegetables, like onions, garlic, and potatoes, require curing in a dry, well-ventilated area before storage to extend their shelf life.

Ethical Harvesting

Harvesting with gratitude and respect for the plants nurtures a deeper connection to our gardens and the earth. Take only what you need, share surplus with others, and consider leaving some produce for wildlife or for natural reseeding, fostering a cycle of abundance and sustainability.

Expanding Your Harvest Horizon

As you grow in your gardening journey, experimenting with new varieties and extending your growing season through succession planting or protective structures can enrich your harvest experience. Each season brings its own lessons and opportunities for discovery, deepening your understanding of the natural rhythms of growth and maturation.

Harvesting, at its essence, is an act of partnership with nature. It requires patience, observation, and a gentle touch, rewarding us not just with the fruits of our labor but with the satisfaction of a cycle completed and the promise of future growth. As we move through the garden, basket in hand, we're reminded of the simple joy of picking a ripe tomato, the fragrance of fresh basil, and the crisp snap of a green bean. These moments, rich with the flavors of the season, are the heart of gardening, connecting us to the earth and to the cycles of life that sustain us.

STORING VEGETABLES FOR LONGEVITY

After the rewarding labor of harvesting comes the critical task of storing vegetables to ensure their longevity, keeping the garden's bounty fresh and nourishing well beyond the growing season. Proper storage techniques not only preserve the quality and flavor of your vegetables but also reduce food waste, allowing you to enjoy the fruits of your labor for as long as possible. This sub-chapter delves into the principles of vegetable storage, offering strategies to maximize the shelf life of your harvest.

Understanding the Basics of Vegetable Storage

The key to effective storage is understanding the unique needs of different vegetables, which vary widely in terms of temperature, humidity, and light requirements. Some vegetables, like potatoes and onions, prefer cool, dark, dry places, while others, such as leafy greens, need higher humidity and more moderate temperatures.

Temperature and Humidity Control

- **Cool and Dry Storage**: Root vegetables (carrots, beets, potatoes) and alliums (onions, garlic) thrive in cool, dry conditions (around 50-60°F and 60-70% humidity). A basement, garage, or even a cool, dark cabinet can serve as suitable storage spaces.

- **Moderate and Humid Storage**: Vegetables like leafy greens, broccoli, and celery require higher humidity and slightly warmer temperatures. Storing these in perforated plastic bags in the refrigerator's crisper drawer can help maintain optimal humidity.

Specific Storage Tips by Vegetable Type

- **Root Vegetables**: Remove tops to prevent moisture loss and store in a cool, dark place. For long-term storage, consider packing in damp sand or sawdust.

- **Squash and Pumpkins**: Cure for 10-14 days in a warm, dry place, then move to a cooler location (50-55°F). Store on shelves or racks to promote air circulation.

- **Tomatoes**: Store at room temperature until ripe; refrigeration can diminish flavor. For long-term storage, consider canning or drying.

- **Leafy Greens**: Wrap in a damp cloth or paper towel and place in a plastic bag in the fridge. Use within a week for best quality.

- **Cucumbers and Zucchini**: Store in the crisper drawer of the refrigerator, in plastic bags with a paper towel to absorb excess moisture.

Ethylene Producers and Sensitive Vegetables

Ethylene gas, produced by some fruits and vegetables as they ripen, can accelerate spoilage in ethylene-sensitive produce. Store ethylene-producing items (like apples and tomatoes) away from sensitive vegetables (like leafy greens and potatoes) to prevent premature ripening or spoilage.

Innovative Storage Solutions

- **Vacuum Sealing**: For vegetables you plan to freeze, vacuum sealing can significantly extend their freezer life by removing air and preventing freezer burn.
- **Refrigeration Alternatives**: For homes without ample refrigerator space, explore alternatives like Zeer pots (evaporative coolers) or root cellars that leverage natural cooling.

Regular Monitoring and Rotation

Check stored vegetables regularly for signs of spoilage, such as soft spots or mold, and remove any affected items to prevent the spread. Rotate your stock, using older vegetables first, to ensure nothing goes to waste.

The Impact of Proper Storage

Beyond extending the life of your harvest, proper storage practices play a crucial role in sustaining your household's food security and reducing dependency on out-of-season imports. By optimizing storage conditions, you harness the full potential of your garden, turning seasonal abundance into year-round sustenance.

Preserving the Connection to Your Garden

Storing vegetables with care is more than a post-harvest necessity—it's a way to honor the time, effort, and love invested in your garden. Each stored vegetable carries the story of its growth from seed to harvest, a tangible link to the sunny days and rich soil that nurtured it. Through thoughtful storage, we extend the lifecycle of our produce, ensuring that the joy and fulfillment of the gardening season enrich our tables and our lives, no matter the season.

In mastering the art of vegetable storage, we not only maximize the longevity of our harvest but also deepen our connection to the cycles of nature. We become participants in a tradition of preservation that spans generations, learning to live in harmony with the rhythms of growth and dormancy that define the natural world.

Basic Preservation Methods: Canning, Freezing, Drying

The cycle of the garden doesn't end at harvest; it extends into the realm of preservation, where the bounty of today is transformed into the comfort of tomorrow. In this sub-chapter, we explore the foundational pillars of preservation: canning, freezing, and drying. These methods, each with its unique charm and technique, offer pathways to savor the flavors of the garden long after its peak has passed. They are acts of anticipation, patience, and respect for the harvest, ensuring that nothing goes to waste and that every meal can carry a taste of the sun-soaked days of growth.

Canning: Capturing Seasons in a Jar

Canning is a method steeped in tradition, a way to lock in the freshness and taste of produce at its peak. It involves processing food in airtight, sterilized containers to extend its shelf life, offering a bridge between abundance and necessity.

- **Water Bath Canning** is suitable for high-acid foods like tomatoes, fruits, jams, jellies, and pickles. This method uses a large pot of boiling water to process jars, ensuring they're sealed and preserved safely.
- **Pressure Canning** is essential for low-acid foods such as vegetables, meats, and soups. It requires a specialized pressure canner to achieve the high temperatures needed to safely preserve these items.

Key Considerations:

- Sterilization of jars and lids is paramount to prevent contamination.
- Understanding the acidity of your produce is crucial; it dictates the canning method required.
- Always leave the appropriate headspace in jars to allow for expansion during processing.

Freezing: Simplicity Meets Efficiency

Freezing is perhaps the most accessible preservation method, preserving the texture, taste, and nutritional value of almost any garden produce. It's a straightforward approach: prepare, pack, and freeze.

- **Blanching** is a pre-freezing technique for vegetables, involving a brief immersion in boiling water followed by cooling in ice water. This process halts enzyme activity that can degrade quality over time.
- **Packing** can be done in rigid containers or freezer bags, depending on the food. Removing as much air as possible will prevent freezer burn and preserve quality.

Advantages:
- Freezing maintains a closer texture and nutritional profile to fresh produce.
- It offers flexibility; you can freeze in portions suitable for your needs.

Drying: The Essence of Simplicity

Drying, one of the oldest food preservation methods, reduces the moisture content in foods, inhibiting the growth of bacteria, yeasts, and molds. Dried foods are lightweight, space-efficient, and imbued with concentrated flavors.

- **Air Drying** is the simplest method, ideal for herbs and hot, dry climates. Hang bunches of herbs or place items on racks in a dry, well-ventilated area.
- **Oven Drying** is more controlled and can be used for a variety of produce, including fruits, vegetables, and herbs. Low temperatures and slightly open oven doors ensure gentle, even drying.
- **Dehydrators** offer the most consistent results, especially for high-moisture items like tomatoes or berries. These devices circulate warm, dry air through food trays, efficiently removing moisture.

Tips for Success:
- Pre-treat certain fruits (like apples and peaches) with lemon juice or ascorbic acid solutions to preserve color and vitamin content.
- Store dried foods in airtight containers in a cool, dark place to maximize shelf life.

The Rhythm of Preservation

Canning, freezing, and drying are not just methods; they are meditations on the cycle of the garden, reflections on the rhythm of seasons and the passage of time. They teach us patience, prompt us to savor the moment, and remind us of the abundance that surrounds us. Each jar of pickles, each bag of frozen peas, each jar of dried herbs carries within it the story of the season, the care of the gardener, and the promise of future meals shared with loved ones.

Embracing the Legacy

As we engage in these acts of preservation, we connect with generations past, drawing on the wisdom and experience of those who have tended the earth and harvested its bounty before us. We learn that to preserve food is to preserve a way of life—one rooted in awareness, gratitude, and respect for the natural world.

Through canning, freezing, and drying, we honor the gifts of the garden, ensuring that its beauty and nourishment continue to enrich our lives, season after season. In this way, preservation becomes more than a practical necessity; it becomes a celebration of the garden's generous spirit, a testament to the enduring connection between land and table.

CREATING A ROOT CELLAR

In the cycle of the garden, the creation of a root cellar is a nod to tradition, an embrace of simplicity, and a testament to sustainability. It's a space dedicated to the earth's natural insulation, where the cool, steady temperatures and controlled humidity extend the life of harvested produce through the winter months. This sub-chapter delves into the principles and practices of creating a root cellar, transforming a corner of the earth into a sanctuary for preservation.

The Essence of a Root Cellar

A root cellar is more than just a storage space; it's a carefully calibrated environment designed to keep vegetables and fruits fresh without the need for electricity. The key elements—temperature, humidity, and ventilation—are managed naturally, drawing on the earth's consistent underground climate.

Choosing the Right Location

- **Underground Advantage**: The ideal root cellar location is partially or entirely below ground where temperatures remain stable.

- **Accessibility**: Consider proximity to your home for easy access during winter months. Adjacent to a basement or under a porch can be convenient options.
- **Drainage**: Ensure the site has good drainage to prevent water accumulation, which can lead to mold and spoilage.

Constructing Your Root Cellar

- **Insulation**: While the earth provides natural insulation, additional insulation may be necessary in colder climates to prevent freezing. Straw bales or rigid foam insulation can enhance thermal stability.
- **Ventilation**: Proper ventilation is crucial to regulate temperature and remove ethylene gas. Incorporate a venting system that allows for air exchange without letting in warmth or pests.
- **Moisture Control**: High humidity is essential for keeping produce from drying out. Earth floors, or adding bins of water, can help maintain humidity levels. However, too much moisture can encourage mold, so balance is key.

Design Considerations

- **Size and Shelving**: Tailor the size of your root cellar to your storage needs, keeping in mind the types of produce you plan to store. Built-in shelving, bins, and racks can maximize space and organization.
- **Lighting**: Minimal lighting is necessary, as most root cellar storage items require darkness. Battery-operated or solar-powered lights can provide illumination without affecting the cellar's environment.

Stocking Your Cellar

- **Produce Selection**: Not all vegetables are suitable for root cellar storage. Root vegetables (carrots, potatoes, beets), hardy fruits (apples, pears), and certain cabbages thrive in the cool, humid conditions.
- **Preparation**: Before storing, cure root vegetables and onions to toughen their skins. Avoid washing produce before storage to minimize moisture.
- **Organization**: Separate produce by type and variety, noting their ideal storage conditions. Some fruits, like apples, produce ethylene gas, which can accelerate ripening and spoilage in vegetables.

Maintenance and Monitoring

- **Regular Checks**: Inspect stored produce regularly for signs of spoilage or disease and remove any compromised items to prevent them from affecting the rest.
- **Temperature and Humidity Logs**: Keep records of temperature and humidity levels to ensure they remain within optimal ranges, making adjustments to ventilation or insulation as needed.

Embracing the Tradition

The creation of a root cellar is a journey back to basics, to a time when seasonal rhythms dictated the ebb and flow of life. It's a practice steeped in the wisdom of ancestors who understood the value of the earth's natural refrigeration.

The Root Cellar's Place in Modern Gardening

In today's world, where convenience often trumps sustainability, the root cellar stands as a symbol of self-sufficiency and environmental stewardship. It represents a commitment to preserving not just food, but also traditional knowledge and a slower, more thoughtful way of living.

A root cellar is more than a structure; it's a bridge between past and present, a space where the bounty of the garden is cradled in the earth's embrace, waiting to nourish us through the winter months. In building a root cellar, we connect with the land in a profound way, reaffirming our role as caretakers of the earth and beneficiaries of its abundance. This sub-chapter not only guides you through creating a functional root cellar but also invites you to partake in a tradition that enriches your garden, your table, and your connection to the natural world.

CONCLUSION

As we bring our journey through **Harvesting, Storing, and Preserving** to a close, we find ourselves rich in knowledge and abundant in yield, standing at the precipice of a bountiful horizon. This chapter has been a deep dive into the culmination of our gardening efforts, where the fruits of our labor finally come into our hands, and the cycle of growth reaches its fulfilling end. Yet, as we conclude, we recognize that this end is but the beginning of another vital phase in our relationship with the garden and its bounty.

A Celebration of Harvest

Harvesting is the gardener's celebration, a time-honored ritual that connects us to the earth and its generous nature. We've explored the signs of ripeness, the techniques for gentle extraction, and the timing that ensures peak flavor and nutrition. This knowledge arms us with the ability to approach our gardens with a discerning eye, transforming the act of harvesting into a dialogue between gardener and plant, a final act of care in the lifecycle of our crops.

The Art of Storing

The wisdom of storing, an ancient art as crucial as the cultivation itself, has unfolded before us. We've delved into methods that extend the life of our harvest, allowing us to savor the garden's abundance long after the growing season has passed. From temperature and humidity considerations to the selection of storage mediums, these strategies are not just about prolonging shelf life but about honoring the produce, ensuring that none of the garden's gifts are lost to time or neglect.

Preserving the Essence

Preserving is perhaps the most transformative aspect of this chapter, where we've learned to capture the essence of our gardens in jars, bottles, and freezers. Through canning, freezing, drying, and fermenting, we've discovered how to carry the flavors of summer into the colder months, creating a pantry that is both a testament to our labor and a source of nourishment and comfort. This section has not just been about techniques but about creating a legacy of taste and health for our families and communities.

A Legacy of Abundance

In concluding **Harvesting, Storing, and Preserving**, we stand back and behold the legacy of abundance our gardens offer. This chapter has equipped us with the skills to ensure that no part of our harvest goes to waste, empowering us to feed our families, share with our neighbors, and contribute to our communities. But beyond the practical, it has reminded us of the deep satisfaction found in the cycle of the garden—a cycle of preparation, growth, harvest, and renewal.

As we move forward, let us carry the lessons of this chapter with us, applying them not just in our gardens but in our lives, nurturing a sustainable, mindful approach to the abundance we cultivate. Let us celebrate every harvest as a symbol of our connection to the earth, a connection that sustains, enriches, and inspires us throughout the seasons.

BOOK 9: FROM GARDEN TO TABLE

The journey from garden to table is a celebration of the cycle of life, a testament to the connection between the earth and the sustenance it provides. In this chapter, we delve into the heart of what it means to bring the bounty of your garden directly into your kitchen and onto your plate. This transition is not merely a matter of harvesting and eating; it's an art form that honors the flavors, textures, and nutrients of home-grown produce, transforming them into meals that nourish both body and soul. Gardening, at its essence, is an act of cultivation—of plants, certainly, but also of wellness, community, and culinary creativity. The act of growing your own food is deeply empowering, providing a tangible connection to the earth and the cycles that sustain life. But the harvest is just the beginning. The true magic happens when these ingredients are crafted into dishes that reflect the care, attention, and love with which they were grown.

Preparing Your Harvest for Cooking

The transition from soil to supper involves more than simply picking and plating; it's a process that starts with knowing when each vegetable, fruit, or herb is at its peak for culinary use. This section will guide you through cleaning, preparing, and preserving your harvest with techniques that enhance flavor and retain nutritional value, ensuring that every bite is a celebration of freshness.

Healthy and Delicious Vegetable Recipes

Here, we will explore a collection of recipes designed to spotlight the natural flavors of your garden's produce. From simple, rustic dishes that let the ingredients shine to more complex creations that weave together textures and tastes, these recipes are meant to inspire both seasoned cooks and culinary novices alike. Whether you're looking for ways to use an abundance of zucchini or searching for the perfect tomato sauce recipe, you'll find ideas here that bring your garden's offerings to vibrant life.

Herbal Infusions and Benefits

Herbs are the unsung heroes of the garden, offering a bounty of flavors, medicinal benefits, and aromatic pleasures. This section introduces the art of creating herbal infusions, teas, and tinctures, unlocking the potent properties of herbs in ways that soothe, invigorate, and heal. Discover how to harness the power of herbs to enhance your well-being and bring a touch of the garden's essence into your daily routines.

Celebrating Your Bounty: Hosting a Garden-to-Table Dinner

The ultimate expression of the garden-to-table journey is the sharing of your harvest with others. Here, we'll discuss how to plan and host a garden-to-table dinner that showcases the richness of your garden. From setting a table that reflects the beauty of the outdoors to crafting a menu that tells a story of growth and community, these gatherings are an opportunity to celebrate the fruits of your labor in the company of friends and family.

The path from garden to table is rich with possibility, a journey that encompasses not only the physical act of growing and cooking but also the emotional and spiritual connections we forge with the food we eat and the earth that nurtures it. This chapter is an invitation to embrace the fullness of that journey, to explore the myriad ways in which the garden enriches our lives and to find joy in the simple act of feeding ourselves and our loved ones with food grown from our own hands and hearts.

PREPARING YOUR HARVEST FOR COOKING

Bringing the harvest from garden to kitchen is a journey that transforms raw, earthy bounty into culinary delights. This process begins with the careful preparation of your harvest for cooking, a step that bridges the gap between the soil and the supper table. Here, we delve into the essential techniques and thoughtful considerations involved in preparing garden-fresh produce, ensuring that every meal celebrates the flavors, textures, and nutritional richness of your home-grown ingredients.

Cleaning and Inspecting Your Harvest

The first step in preparing your harvest is a thorough cleaning to remove soil, pests, and any residues from the garden. Gentle washing under running water suffices for most vegetables and fruits, though a soft brush can help dislodge dirt from root vegetables. Leafy greens might require multiple rinses in a large basin of water to remove grit fully.

- **Inspect as You Clean**: This is also the perfect time to inspect your produce for signs of damage, disease, or pests. Removing affected areas ensures that only the best quality produce makes it to your table.

The Art of Trimming and Preparing

Each type of produce demands specific preparation techniques to maximize its culinary potential and nutritional value.

- **Leafy Greens**: Remove any wilted or discolored leaves. For greens with thicker stems, like kale, strip the leaves from the stems unless the recipe calls for whole leaves.
- **Root Vegetables**: Peel or scrub root vegetables according to the dish's needs. Some skins, like those on carrots and potatoes, are nutritious and flavorful when left on, provided they're well-cleaned.
- **Herbs**: Pluck leaves from stems for most herbs, except when they're tender and the recipe calls for whole sprigs. Chopping or tearing herbs is best done just before adding them to your dish to preserve their essential oils.

Cutting Techniques to Enhance Flavor and Cooking

How you cut your produce can affect both its cooking properties and flavor profile. Uniform pieces not only cook more evenly but can also enhance a dish's visual appeal.

- **Dicing and Slicing**: Uniform dicing or slicing is crucial for even cooking. Consider the size based on cooking time and how they'll integrate with other ingredients.
- **Julienning**: This technique, involving cutting into long, thin strips, is perfect for stir-fries or garnishes, allowing for quick cooking and delicate texture.

Blanching and Shocking: Preserving Color and Texture

Blanching—briefly boiling vegetables and then plunging them into ice water (shocking)—is a technique used to preserve vibrant colors, halt enzyme actions that can lead to spoilage, and tenderize tougher vegetables. It's especially useful for green vegetables like broccoli and green beans, ensuring they maintain their crispness and hue.

The Importance of Tasting and Seasoning

- **Taste as You Go**: The freshness of garden produce means flavors can be more intense or varied. Taste your vegetables at different preparation stages to adjust seasoning and cooking times as needed.
- **Seasoning**: Fresh herbs, salt, and pepper can enhance the natural flavors of your vegetables. Season lightly before cooking and adjust before serving.

Storing Prepared Produce

If you're not cooking immediately after preparation, proper storage is key to maintaining freshness:

- **Refrigeration**: Store prepared vegetables in airtight containers or wrapped in damp paper towels inside sealable bags in the refrigerator.
- **Herbs**: Wrap prepared herbs in damp paper towels and place them in airtight containers, or keep stems in a jar of water, loosely covered with a plastic bag.

Mindful Preparation: The Gateway to Flavorful Meals

Preparing your harvest for cooking is an act of mindfulness, a moment to appreciate the journey from seed to plate. This stage of the garden-to-table process is where creativity begins, influencing the texture, flavor, and nutritional value of the dishes you create. Through thoughtful preparation, we pay homage to the produce, ensuring that each vegetable or fruit can express its fullest potential in the meals we share.

The transition from garden to kitchen is filled with anticipation and possibility. Each step in preparing your harvest for cooking—from washing and trimming to cutting and blanching—contributes to the alchemy that turns simple ingredients into nourishing, delicious meals. This journey underscores the profound connection between gardener and chef, earth and table, reinforcing the idea that the food we grow and how we prepare it can deeply enrich our lives. In embracing these preparation practices, we celebrate not just the flavors of the garden but the joy and satisfaction of feeding ourselves and our loved ones with care, creativity, and respect for the natural world.

HEALTHY AND DELICIOUS VEGETABLE RECIPES

In this collection, we dive into a world where the garden's abundance meets the kitchen's creativity, crafting recipes that highlight the best of what the season has to offer. These dishes are designed not just to nourish but to inspire, with flavors that speak of the care and passion poured into every garden bed. From vibrant salads and hearty soups to innovative main courses, each recipe brings the freshness of the garden directly to your table, promising meals that are both healthy and delicious. Emphasizing simplicity and the natural beauty of vegetables, these recipes are a testament to the joy of garden-to-table eating, where every ingredient tells a story of sunlight, soil, and care.

ROASTED BEET AND QUINOA SALAD

PREPARATION TIME: 20 min - **COOKING TIME:** 45 min **MODE OF COOKING:** Roasting and Boiling - **INGREDIENTS:**

- 4 medium beets, peeled and cubed
- 1 cup quinoa
- 2 cups water
- 1/4 cup olive oil
- 2 Tbsp apple cider vinegar
- 1 Tbsp honey
- 1/4 cup feta cheese, crumbled
- 1/4 cup walnuts, toasted and chopped
- Salt and pepper to taste
- Mixed greens for serving

DIRECTIONS:

1. Preheat oven to 375°F (190°C). Toss beets with 1 Tbsp. olive oil, salt, and pepper. Spread on a baking sheet and roast until tender, about 45 min.

2. Rinse quinoa under cold water. In a medium saucepan, bring quinoa and water to a boil. Reduce heat to low, cover, and simmer until water is absorbed, about 15 min. Let cool.

3. In a small bowl, whisk together remaining olive oil, apple cider vinegar, honey, salt, and pepper to create the dressing.

4. In a large bowl, combine roasted beets, cooked quinoa, feta cheese, and walnuts. Pour dressing over the salad and toss to combine.

5. Serve over a bed of mixed greens.

TIPS:

- For an extra crunch, add sunflower seeds.
- Goat cheese can be used in place of feta for a creamier texture.

N.V.: Calories: 350, Fat: 15g, Carbs: 45g, Protein: 10g, Sugar: 12g

---

CREAMY CARROT SOUP WITH GINGER

PREPARATION TIME: 10 min - **COOKING TIME:** 30 min **MODE OF COOKING:** Simmering - **INGREDIENTS:**

- 1 lb carrots, peeled and chopped
- 1 large onion, chopped
- 2 Tbsp ginger, minced
- 2 cloves garlic, minced
- 4 cups vegetable broth
- 1 cup coconut milk
- 2 Tbsp olive oil
- Salt and pepper to taste
- Pumpkin seeds for garnish

DIRECTIONS:

1. In a large pot, heat olive oil over medium heat. Add onion, garlic, and ginger, sautéing until onion is translucent.

2. Add chopped carrots and vegetable broth. Bring to a boil, then reduce heat and simmer until carrots are tender, about 20 min.

3. Use an immersion blender to purée the soup until smooth. Stir in coconut milk and season with salt and pepper.

4. Serve hot, garnished with pumpkin seeds.

TIPS:

- For a spicier soup, add a pinch of cayenne pepper.

- Serve with a dollop of yogurt for added creaminess.

N.V.: Calories: 220, Fat: 14g, Carbs: 24g, Protein: 3g, Sugar: 11g

---

GRILLED EGGPLANT WITH HERBED QUINOA

PREPARATION TIME: 20 min - **COOKING TIME:** 30 min **MODE OF COOKING:** Grilling **INGREDIENTS:**

- 2 medium eggplants, sliced into 1/2-inch rounds

- 1 cup quinoa, rinsed

- 2 cups vegetable broth

- 1/4 cup fresh parsley, chopped

- 1/4 cup fresh basil, chopped

- 2 Tbsp. olive oil

- 2 Tbsp. lemon juice

- Salt and pepper to taste

DIRECTIONS:

1. Preheat grill to medium-high heat.

2. Brush eggplant slices with olive oil and season with salt and pepper. Grill until tender and slightly charred, about 5 min per side.

3. Meanwhile, bring quinoa and vegetable broth to a boil in a medium saucepan. Reduce heat, cover, and simmer for 15 min or until liquid is absorbed.

4. Remove from heat, fluff with a fork, and stir in parsley, basil, lemon juice, and a drizzle of olive oil.

5. Serve grilled eggplant over a bed of herbed quinoa.

TIPS:

- For a smoky flavor, char the lemon on the grill before juicing.

- Add grilled cherry tomatoes for a pop of sweetness.

N.V.: Calories: 310, Fat: 10g, Carbs: 49g, Protein: 8g, Sugar: 5g

---

SPICY KALE AND SWEET POTATO SOUP

PREPARATION TIME: 15 min - **COOKING TIME:** 30 min **MODE OF COOKING:** Simmering -**INGREDIENTS:**

- 1 Tbsp. olive oil
- 1 onion, diced
- 2 cloves garlic, minced
- 1 tsp ground cumin
- 1/2 tsp smoked paprika
- 1/4 tsp cayenne pepper
- 2 large sweet potatoes, peeled and cubed
- 6 cups vegetable broth
- 4 cups kale, stems removed and leaves torn
- Salt and pepper to taste

DIRECTIONS:

1. Heat olive oil in a large pot over medium heat. Add onion and garlic, cooking until soft.
2. Stir in cumin, paprika, and cayenne, cooking for 1 min.
3. Add sweet potatoes and vegetable broth. Bring to a boil, then reduce heat and simmer until potatoes are tender, about 20 min.
4. Add kale and cook until wilted, about 5 min. Season with salt and pepper.
5. Use an immersion blender to partially puree the soup, leaving some chunks for texture.

TIPS:

- Serve with a dollop of Greek yogurt and a sprinkle of chili flakes for extra heat.
- Top with roasted pumpkin seeds for crunch.

N.V.: Calories: 180, Fat: 3g, Carbs: 35g, Protein: 4g, Sugar: 6g

ROASTED BEET AND GOAT CHEESE SALAD

PREPARATION TIME: 15 min - **COOKING TIME:** 1 hr **MODE OF COOKING:** Roasting - **INGREDIENTS:**

- 4 medium beets, scrubbed
- 1/4 cup walnuts, chopped
- 1/4 cup crumbled goat cheese
- 2 cups mixed salad greens
- 2 Tbsp. balsamic vinegar
- 1 Tbsp. olive oil
- Salt and pepper to taste

DIRECTIONS:

1. Preheat oven to 400°F (200°C). Wrap beets in foil and roast until tender, about 1 hr.
2. Once cooled, peel and slice the beets.
3. Arrange salad greens on plates and top with sliced beets, walnuts, and goat cheese.
4. Whisk together balsamic vinegar and olive oil, drizzle over salad, and season with salt and pepper.

TIPS:

- For added sweetness, drizzle with honey before serving.
- Toast walnuts for a deeper flavor.

N.V.: Calories: 220, Fat: 15g, Carbs: 18g, Protein: 6g, Sugar: 13g

GRILLED EGGPLANT WITH HERBED QUINOA

PREPARATION TIME: 20 min - **COOKING TIME:** 30 min

MODE OF COOKING: Grilling

INGREDIENTS:

- 2 medium eggplants, sliced into 1/2-inch rounds
- 2 Tbsp olive oil
- 1 cup quinoa, rinsed

- 2 cups vegetable broth
- 1/4 cup fresh parsley, chopped
- 1/4 cup fresh mint, chopped
- 1 lemon, juiced
- Salt and pepper to taste

DIRECTIONS:

1. Preheat the grill to medium-high heat (about 375°F or 190°C). Brush both sides of the eggplant slices with olive oil and season with salt and pepper.
2. Grill eggplant slices for 5 minutes on each side, or until tender and grill marks appear.
3. Meanwhile, in a saucepan, bring quinoa and vegetable broth to a boil. Reduce heat to low, cover, and simmer for 15 minutes, or until liquid is absorbed.
4. Fluff quinoa with a fork and stir in parsley, mint, and lemon juice. Season with salt and pepper to taste.
5. Serve grilled eggplant on a bed of herbed quinoa.

TIPS:

- For a smoky flavor, char the lemon on the grill before juicing.
- Quinoa can be prepared ahead of time and served cold or gently reheated.

N.V.: Calories: 300, Fat: 10g, Carbs: 45g, Protein: 8g, Sugar: 5g

---

ZUCCHINI FRITTERS

PREPARATION TIME: 15 min - **COOKING TIME:** 15 min

MODE OF COOKING: Frying

INGREDIENTS:

- 2 medium zucchinis, grated
- 1/2 cup all-purpose flour
- 1/4 cup grated Parmesan cheese
- 2 cloves garlic, minced
- 1 egg, beaten
- 2 Tbsp. chopped fresh parsley
- Salt and pepper to taste

- Olive oil for frying

PROCEDURE:

1. Place grated zucchini in a clean kitchen towel and squeeze out excess moisture.
2. In a large bowl, combine grated zucchini, flour, Parmesan cheese, minced garlic, beaten egg, chopped parsley, salt, and pepper. Mix until well combined.
3. Heat olive oil in a skillet over medium heat.
4. Drop spoonsful of the zucchini mixture into the hot oil and flatten slightly with the back of the spoon.
5. Fry for 3-4 minutes on each side, until golden brown and crispy.
6. Remove from the skillet and drain on paper towels. Serve hot with your favorite dipping sauce.

NUTRITIONAL VALUES: Calories: 160, Fat: 6g, Carbs: 21g, Protein: 7g, Sugar: 2g

---

ZUCCHINI NOODLES WITH PESTO

PREPARATION TIME: 10 min - **COOKING TIME:** 5 min

MODE OF COOKING: Sauteing

INGREDIENTS:

- 2 medium zucchinis, spiralized into noodles
- 1/4 cup basil pesto
- 1 Tbsp. olive oil
- Salt and pepper to taste
- Grated Parmesan cheese for garnish

PROCEDURE:

1. Heat olive oil in a skillet over medium heat.
2. Add zucchini noodles to the skillet and sauté for 2-3 minutes, until just tender.
3. Stir in basil pesto and toss until zucchini noodles are evenly coated.
4. Season with salt and pepper to taste.
5. Remove from heat and transfer to serving plates.
6. Garnish with grated Parmesan cheese before serving.

NUTRITIONAL VALUES: Calories: 250, Fat: 22g, Carbs: 8g, Protein: 7g, Sugar: 4g

STUFFED ZUCCHINI BOATS

PREPARATION TIME: 20 min - **COOKING TIME:** 25 min

MODE OF COOKING:

Baking

INGREDIENTS:

- 4 medium zucchinis, halved lengthwise
- 1 cup cooked quinoa
- 1/2 cup cherry tomatoes, halved
- 1/2 cup crumbled feta cheese
- 2 Tbsp. chopped fresh basil
- 2 cloves garlic, minced
- 1 Tbsp. olive oil
- Salt and pepper to taste

PROCEDURE:

1. Preheat oven to 375°F (190°C).
2. Using a spoon, scoop out the flesh from the zucchini halves, leaving about 1/4-inch-thick shells.
3. In a mixing bowl, combine the scooped zucchini flesh, cooked quinoa, cherry tomatoes, crumbled feta cheese, chopped basil, minced garlic, olive oil, salt, and pepper. Mix until well combined.
4. Stuff the mixture into the hollowed-out zucchini halves.
5. Place the stuffed zucchini boats on a baking sheet lined with parchment paper.

6. Bake in the preheated oven for 20-25 minutes, or until the zucchini is tender and the filling is heated through.

7. Serve hot, garnished with additional chopped basil if desired.

NUTRITIONAL VALUES: Calories: 180, Fat: 9g, Carbs: 20g, Protein: 7g, Sugar: 4g

---

ZUCCHINI AND CORN SALAD

PREPARATION TIME: 10 min - **COOKING TIME:** 5 min

MODE OF COOKING: Raw

INGREDIENTS:

- 2 medium zucchinis, diced
- 1 cup fresh corn kernels
- 1/4 cup diced red onion
- 1/4 cup chopped fresh cilantro
- 1 jalapeno pepper, seeded and diced
- Juice of 1 lime
- 2 Tbsp. olive oil
- Salt and pepper to taste
- Avocado slices for garnish (optional)

PROCEDURE:

1. In a large bowl, combine diced zucchini, fresh corn kernels, diced red onion, chopped cilantro, and diced jalapeno pepper.

2. Drizzle lime juice and olive oil over the salad. Toss until evenly coated.

3. Season with salt and pepper to taste.

4. Let the salad marinate in the refrigerator for at least 30 minutes before serving.

5. Serve chilled, garnished with avocado slices if desired.

NUTRITIONAL VALUES: Calories: 140, Fat: 8g, Carbs: 17g, Protein: 3g, Sugar: 6g

---

RECIPE 5: ZUCCHINI AND FETA QUICHE

PREPARATION TIME: 20 min - **COOKING TIME:** 40 min

MODE OF COOKING: Baking

INGREDIENTS:

- 1 prepared pie crust
- 2 medium zucchinis, thinly sliced
- 1 cup crumbled feta cheese
- 1/2 cup chopped fresh spinach
- 1/4 cup chopped sun-dried tomatoes
- 4 eggs
- 1 cup milk
- Salt and pepper to taste

PROCEDURE:

1. Preheat oven to 375°F (190°C).
2. Place the prepared pie crust in a pie dish and crimp the edges.
3. Layer sliced zucchini, crumbled feta cheese, chopped spinach, and sun-dried tomatoes in the pie crust.
4. In a mixing bowl, whisk together eggs and milk until well combined. Season with salt and pepper.
5. Pour the egg mixture over the zucchini and feta cheese filling in the pie crust.
6. Bake in the preheated oven for 35-40 minutes, or until the quiche is set and golden brown on top.
7. Remove from the oven and let cool for a few minutes before slicing and serving.

NUTRITIONAL VALUES: Calories: 320, Fat: 20g, Carbs: 23g, Protein: 14g

---

ZUCCHINI CHOCOLATE CHIP MUFFINS

PREPARATION TIME: 15 min - **COOKING TIME:** 20 min

MODE OF COOKING: Baking

INGREDIENTS:

- 2 cups all-purpose flour
- 1/2 cup granulated sugar
- 1/4 cup brown sugar
- 1 tsp baking powder
- 1/2 tsp baking soda

- 1/2 tsp salt
- 1/2 tsp ground cinnamon
- 2 large eggs
- 1/2 cup vegetable oil
- 1/4 cup milk
- 1 tsp vanilla extract
- 1 cup shredded zucchini, excess moisture squeezed out
- 3/4 cup chocolate chips

PROCEDURE:

1. Preheat oven to 350°F (175°C). Line a muffin tin with paper liners.
2. In a large bowl, whisk together flour, granulated sugar, brown sugar, baking powder, baking soda, salt, and ground cinnamon.
3. In another bowl, beat eggs, vegetable oil, milk, and vanilla extract until well combined.
4. Stir shredded zucchini into the wet ingredients.
5. Add the wet ingredients to the dry ingredients and mix until just combined. Fold in chocolate chips.
6. Divide the batter evenly among the muffin cups, filling each about 3/4 full.
7. Bake in the preheated oven for 18-20 minutes, or until a toothpick inserted into the center comes out clean.
8. Remove from the oven and let cool in the muffin tin for 5 minutes before transferring to a wire rack to cool completely.

NUTRITIONAL VALUES: Calories: 250, Fat: 12g, Carbs: 34g, Protein: 4g, Sugar: 18g

ZUCCHINI AND TOMATO PASTA

PREPARATION TIME: 10 min - **COOKING TIME:** 20 min

MODE OF COOKING: Sauteing

INGREDIENTS:

- 8 oz. spaghetti or pasta of choice
- 2 medium zucchinis, thinly sliced

- 2 cups cherry tomatoes, halved
- 3 cloves garlic, minced
- 1/4 cup chopped fresh basil
- 2 Tbsp. olive oil
- Salt and pepper to taste
- Grated Parmesan cheese for serving

PROCEDURE:

1. Cook spaghetti according to package instructions until al dente. Drain and set aside.
2. In a large skillet, heat olive oil over medium heat.
3. Add minced garlic and cook until fragrant, about 1 minute.
4. Add thinly sliced zucchinis to the skillet and sauté until tender, about 5-6 minutes.
5. Stir in cherry tomatoes and cook for an additional 2-3 minutes, until tomatoes are slightly softened.
6. Add cooked spaghetti to the skillet along with chopped fresh basil. Toss until well combined.
7. Season with salt and pepper to taste.
8. Serve hot, garnished with grated Parmesan cheese.

NUTRITIONAL VALUES: Calories: 320, Fat: 10g, Carbs: 50g, Protein: 10g, Sugar: 5g

---

ZUCCHINI AND POTATO HASH

PREPARATION TIME: 15 min - **COOKING TIME:** 20 min

MODE OF COOKING: Sauteing

INGREDIENTS:

- 2 medium zucchinis, diced
- 2 medium potatoes, peeled and diced
- 1/2 onion, diced
- 2 cloves garlic, minced
- 2 Tbsp. olive oil

- 1 tsp paprika
- Salt and pepper to taste
- Chopped fresh parsley for garnish

PROCEDURE:

1. Heat olive oil in a large skillet over medium heat.
2. Add diced potatoes to the skillet and cook until golden and crispy, about 8-10 minutes.
3. Add diced zucchinis, diced onion, and minced garlic to the skillet. Cook until vegetables are tender, about 5-6 minutes.
4. Sprinkle paprika over the hash and season with salt and pepper to taste. Stir to combine.
5. Cook for an additional 2-3 minutes, allowing the flavors to meld together.
6. Remove from heat and garnish with chopped fresh parsley before serving.

NUTRITIONAL VALUES: Calories: 220, Fat: 8g, Carbs: 35g, Protein: 5g, Sugar: 5g

---

ZUCCHINI AND BLACK BEAN QUESADILLAS

PREPARATION TIME: 10 min - **COOKING TIME:** 10 min

MODE OF COOKING: Pan-frying

INGREDIENTS:

- 4 large flour tortillas
- 1 cup shredded Monterey Jack cheese
- 1 cup canned black beans, drained and rinsed
- 1 medium zucchini, thinly sliced
- 1/2 cup salsa
- 1/4 cup chopped fresh cilantro
- 2 Tbsp. olive oil

PROCEDURE:

1. Place a tortilla on a flat surface. Sprinkle shredded Monterey Jack cheese evenly over half of the tortilla.
2. Layer sliced zucchini and black beans over the cheese.
3. Spoon salsa over the top and sprinkle with chopped fresh cilantro.

4. Fold the tortilla in half to cover the filling, pressing down gently to seal.

5. Repeat with the remaining tortillas and filling ingredients.

6. Heat olive oil in a large skillet over medium heat.

7. Place filled quesadillas in the skillet and cook for 3-4 minutes on each side, until golden and crispy.

8. Remove from the skillet and let cool for a minute before slicing into wedges.

9. Serve hot, with additional salsa and sour cream if desired.

NUTRITIONAL VALUES: Calories: 380, Fat: 16g, Carbs: 45g, Protein: 14g, Sugar: 3g

EGGPLANT PARMESAN

PREPARATION TIME: 20 min - **COOKING TIME:** 45 min

MODE OF COOKING: Baking

INGREDIENTS:

- 2 large eggplants, sliced into 1/2-inch rounds
- Salt
- 2 cups breadcrumbs
- 1 cup grated Parmesan cheese
- 2 eggs, beaten
- 2 cups marinara sauce
- 2 cups shredded mozzarella cheese
- Fresh basil leaves for garnish

PROCEDURE:

1. Preheat oven to 375°F (190°C). Grease a baking sheet.

2. Place eggplant slices in a colander and sprinkle with salt. Let sit for 20 minutes to draw out excess moisture.

3. Rinse eggplant slices under cold water and pat dry with paper towels.

4. In a shallow dish, combine breadcrumbs and grated Parmesan cheese.

5. Dip each eggplant slice into beaten eggs, then coat with breadcrumb mixture.

6. Place breaded eggplant slices on the prepared baking sheet.

7. Bake in the preheated oven for 20 minutes, or until golden brown and crispy.

8. Spread marinara sauce evenly in the bottom of a baking dish. Place a layer of baked eggplant slices on top of the sauce, followed by a layer of shredded mozzarella cheese. Repeat layers.

9. Bake for an additional 25 minutes, or until the cheese is bubbly and golden.

10. Garnish with fresh basil leaves before serving.

NUTRITIONAL VALUES: Calories: 350, Fat: 15g, Carbs: 35g, Protein: 18g, Sugar: 10g

GRILLED EGGPLANT WITH YOGURT SAUCE

PREPARATION TIME: 15 min -
COOKING TIME: 10 min
MODE OF COOKING: Grilling

INGREDIENTS:

- 2 medium eggplants, sliced lengthwise
- Salt
- 1/4 cup olive oil
- 1/4 cup chopped fresh parsley
- 2 cloves garlic, minced
- Juice of 1 lemon
- Salt and pepper to taste
- 1 cup Greek yogurt
- 1 Tbsp. tahini
- 1 Tbsp. chopped fresh mint

PROCEDURE:

1. Place eggplant slices in a colander and sprinkle with salt. Let sit for 20 minutes to draw out excess moisture.
2. Rinse eggplant slices under cold water and pat dry with paper towels.
3. In a small bowl, whisk together olive oil, chopped fresh parsley, minced garlic, lemon juice, salt, and pepper to make a marinade.
4. Brush both sides of eggplant slices with the marinade.
5. Preheat grill to medium-high heat. Grill eggplant slices for 4-5 minutes on each side, or until tender and grill marks appear.
6. In another small bowl, mix together Greek yogurt, tahini, chopped fresh mint, salt, and pepper to make the sauce.
7. Serve grilled eggplant slices with yogurt sauce drizzled on top.

NUTRITIONAL VALUES: Calories: 250, Fat: 15g, Carbs: 20g, Protein: 10g, Sugar: 10g

EGGPLANT ROLLATINI

PREPARATION TIME: 30 min - **COOKING TIME:** 30 min

MODE OF COOKING: Baking

INGREDIENTS:

- 2 large eggplants, thinly sliced lengthwise
- Salt
- 2 cups ricotta cheese
- 1 cup grated Parmesan cheese
- 1/4 cup chopped fresh basil
- 1 egg, beaten
- 2 cups marinara sauce
- 1 cup shredded mozzarella cheese
- Fresh basil leaves for garnish

PROCEDURE:

1. Preheat oven to 375°F (190°C). Grease a baking dish.
2. Place eggplant slices in a colander and sprinkle with salt. Let sit for 20 minutes to draw out excess moisture.

3. Rinse eggplant slices under cold water and pat dry with paper towels.

4. In a mixing bowl, combine ricotta cheese, grated Parmesan cheese, chopped fresh basil, and beaten egg. Mix until well combined.

5. Spread a spoonful of the cheese mixture onto each eggplant slice, then roll up tightly.

6. Spread marinara sauce evenly in the bottom of the prepared baking dish. Place eggplant rollatini seam side down in the sauce.

7. Top with shredded mozzarella cheese.

8. Bake in the preheated oven for 25-30 minutes, or until the cheese is bubbly and golden.

9. Garnish with fresh basil leaves before serving.

NUTRITIONAL VALUES: Calories: 400, Fat: 20g, Carbs: 30g, Protein: 25g, Sugar: 15g

---

EGGPLANT CAPRESE SALAD

PREPARATION TIME: 15 min - **COOKING TIME:** 10 min

MODE OF COOKING: Grilling

INGREDIENTS:

- 2 medium eggplants, sliced into rounds
- Salt
- 1/4 cup olive oil
- 1 cup cherry tomatoes, halved
- 8 oz. fresh mozzarella cheese, sliced
- 1/4 cup balsamic glaze
- Fresh basil leaves for garnish

PROCEDURE:

1. Place eggplant slices in a colander and sprinkle with salt. Let sit for 20 minutes to draw out excess moisture.

2. Rinse eggplant slices under cold water and pat dry with paper towels.

3. Preheat grill to medium-high heat. Brush eggplant slices with olive oil on both sides.

4. Grill eggplant slices for 3-4 minutes on each side, or until tender and grill marks appear.

5. Arrange grilled eggplant slices on a serving platter.

6. Top each slice with halved cherry tomatoes and a slice of fresh mozzarella cheese.

7. Drizzle balsamic glaze over the top.

8. Garnish with fresh basil leaves before serving.

NUTRITIONAL VALUES: Calories: 320, Fat: 20g, Carbs: 25g, Protein: 15g, Sugar: 15g

---

STUFFED BELL PEPPERS

PREPARATION TIME: 20 min - **COOKING TIME:** 40 min
MODE OF COOKING: Baking
INGREDIENTS:

- 4 large bell peppers, halved and seeded

- 1 cup cooked quinoa

- 1 lb ground beef or turkey

- 1 onion, diced

- 2 cloves garlic, minced

- 1 cup diced tomatoes

- 1 cup shredded cheddar cheese

- 1 tsp dried oregano

- Salt and pepper to taste

- Chopped fresh parsley for garnish

PROCEDURE:

1. Preheat oven to 375°F (190°C). Grease a baking dish.

2. Place bell pepper halves in the prepared baking dish, cut side up.

3. In a skillet, cook ground beef or turkey over medium heat until browned. Drain excess fat.

4. Add diced onion and minced garlic to the skillet. Cook until onion is softened.

5. Stir in cooked quinoa, diced tomatoes, shredded cheddar cheese, dried oregano, salt, and pepper. Cook for another 2-3 minutes.

6. Spoon the quinoa mixture into each bell pepper half, pressing down gently to fill.

7. Cover the baking dish with aluminum foil and bake in the preheated oven for 30 minutes.

8. Remove foil and bake for an additional 10 minutes, or until peppers are tender and filling is heated through.

9. Garnish with chopped fresh parsley before serving.

NUTRITIONAL VALUES: Calories: 380, Fat: 18g, Carbs: 30g, Protein: 25g, Sugar: 8g

---

ROASTED RED PEPPER HUMMUS

PREPARATION TIME: 10 min - **COOKING TIME:** 25 min
MODE OF COOKING: Roasting
INGREDIENTS:

- 2 large red bell peppers
- 1 can (15 oz) chickpeas, drained and rinsed
- 2 cloves garlic, minced
- 1/4 cup tahini
- Juice of 1 lemon
- 2 Tbsp. olive oil
- 1/2 tsp ground cumin
- Salt and pepper to taste
- Chopped fresh parsley for garnish
- Toasted pita bread or vegetables for serving

PROCEDURE:

1. Preheat oven to 425°F (220°C). Line a baking sheet with parchment paper.

2. Place whole red bell peppers on the prepared baking sheet.

3. Roast in the preheated oven for 20-25 minutes, or until peppers are charred and softened.

4. Remove peppers from the oven and transfer to a bowl. Cover with plastic wrap and let steam for 10 minutes.

5. Peel off the charred skin from the peppers and remove the seeds and stems.

6. In a food processor, combine roasted red peppers, chickpeas, minced garlic, tahini, lemon juice, olive oil, ground cumin, salt, and pepper. Blend until smooth and creamy.

7. Transfer hummus to a serving bowl and garnish with chopped fresh parsley.

8. Serve with toasted pita bread or vegetables for dipping.

NUTRITIONAL VALUES: Calories: 180, Fat: 10g, Carbs: 20g, Protein: 6g, Sugar: 3g

GRILLED STUFFED MINI PEPPERS

PREPARATION TIME: 15 min - **COOKING TIME:** 10 min
MODE OF COOKING: Grilling
INGREDIENTS:

- 12 mini sweet peppers, halved and seeded
- 4 oz cream cheese, softened
- 1/4 cup shredded cheddar cheese
- 2 green onions, thinly sliced
- 1/4 tsp garlic powder
- Salt and pepper to taste
- Olive oil for brushing

PROCEDURE:

1. Preheat grill to medium-high heat.

2. In a mixing bowl, combine softened cream cheese, shredded cheddar cheese, sliced green onions, garlic powder, salt, and pepper. Mix until well combined.

3. Stuff each mini pepper half with the cream cheese mixture, pressing down gently to fill.

4. Brush the outside of the stuffed peppers with olive oil.

5. Place stuffed peppers on the preheated grill, cut side down.

6. Grill for 3-4 minutes on each side, or until peppers are charred and filling is heated through.

7. Remove from the grill and serve hot.

NUTRITIONAL VALUES: Calories: 120, Fat: 9g, Carbs: 6g, Protein: 4g, Sugar: 3g

---

CHICKEN FAJITA STUFFED PEPPERS

PREPARATION TIME: 20 min - **COOKING TIME:** 25 min
MODE OF COOKING: Baking
INGREDIENTS:

- 4 large bell peppers, halved and seeded
- 1 lb boneless, skinless chicken breasts, thinly sliced
- 1 onion, thinly sliced
- 1 red bell pepper, thinly sliced
- 1 green bell pepper, thinly sliced
- 2 cloves garlic, minced
- 2 tsp chili powder
- 1 tsp ground cumin
- 1/2 tsp paprika
- Salt and pepper to taste
- 1 cup shredded cheddar cheese
- Chopped fresh cilantro for garnish

PROCEDURE:

1. Preheat oven to 375°F (190°C). Grease a baking dish.

2. Place bell pepper halves in the prepared baking dish, cut side up.

3. In a skillet, heat olive oil over medium-high heat. Add sliced chicken breasts and cook until browned on all sides.

4. Add sliced onion, sliced red bell pepper, sliced green bell pepper, and minced garlic to the skillet. Cook until vegetables are softened.

5. Stir in chili powder, ground cumin, paprika, salt, and pepper. Cook for another 2-3 minutes.

6. Spoon the chicken fajita mixture into each bell pepper half, pressing down gently to fill.

7. Top each stuffed pepper with shredded cheddar cheese.

8. Cover the baking dish with aluminum foil and bake in the preheated oven for 20 minutes.

9. Remove foil and bake for an additional 5 minutes, or until peppers are tender and cheese is melted.

10.   Garnish with chopped fresh cilantro before serving.

NUTRITIONAL VALUES: Calories: 350, Fat: 15g, Carbs: 20g, Protein: 30g, Sugar: 8g

A Garden to Table Delight: Tomato Preserves

Transforming the ripe, sun-kissed tomatoes from your garden into savory preserves is a journey that marries the art of canning with the bounty of the earth. This guide will take you through the steps of making tomato preserves, ensuring that the robust flavors of summer can be savored long after the growing season has passed.

Gathering Your Bounty

The first step in creating tomato preserves is to gather your ripest, most flavorful tomatoes. Look for tomatoes that are firm, with a rich color, and free from bruises or blemishes. The variety of tomato you choose can range from classic beefsteaks to sweet cherry tomatoes, each offering a unique taste profile to your preserves.

Preparing Your Tomatoes

1. **Wash and Dry:** Begin by thoroughly washing your tomatoes to remove any dirt or debris. Gently pat them dry with a clean towel.

2. **Peel the Tomatoes:** To peel, make a small X on the bottom of each tomato with a knife. Blanch the tomatoes by placing them in boiling water for 30-60 seconds, then immediately transfer them to ice water. The skins should slide off easily.

3. **Remove the Seeds (Optional):** For a smoother preserve, cut your tomatoes in quarters and gently squeeze or use a spoon to remove the seeds.

4. **Chop:** Coarsely chop the peeled and seeded tomatoes into uniform pieces to ensure even cooking.

Ingredients and Tools

Before you begin cooking, assemble the following ingredients and tools:

- 5 pounds of prepared tomatoes
- 2 cups sugar (adjust to taste for sweeter or more savory preserves)
- ¼ cup lemon juice
- 1 teaspoon salt
- Optional: herbs or spices such as basil, thyme, or a pinch of red pepper flakes

Tools:

- Large pot
- Canning jars with lids and bands
- Canning funnel
- Ladle
- Jar lifter
- Clean cloth

Cooking Your Tomato Preserves

1. **Combine Ingredients:** In a large pot, combine your chopped tomatoes, sugar, lemon juice, and salt. If desired, add your chosen herbs or spices.

2. **Simmer:** Bring the mixture to a simmer over medium heat, stirring occasionally to prevent sticking. Cook until the mixture thickens, typically around 1 to 2 hours. The preserves should have a glossy appearance and a jam-like consistency.

3. **Taste and Adjust:** Taste your preserves and adjust the seasoning or sugar according to your preference.

Canning Process

While your tomato mixture is cooking, prepare your canning jars.

1. **Sterilize Jars:** Wash your canning jars, lids, and bands in soapy water and rinse well. Then, boil the jars for 10 minutes to sterilize them. Keep the jars in hot water until you're ready to use them.

2. **Fill Jars:** Carefully remove the hot jars from the water. Use a canning funnel to ladle the tomato preserves into the jars, leaving about ½ inch of headspace at the top.

3. **Seal:** Wipe the rims of the jars with a clean cloth to ensure a good seal. Place the lids on the jars and screw the bands on until fingertip tight.

4. **Process:** Process the jars in a boiling water bath for 10-15 minutes. Adjust the time based on your altitude.

5. **Cool:** Remove the jars from the water bath and let them cool on a towel or cooling rack. You should hear a popping sound as the jars seal. Once cool, check the seals by pressing the center of each lid. If the lid doesn't pop back, the jar is sealed.

Storage

Label your jars with the date and store them in a cool, dark place. Properly sealed preserves can last up to a year. Once opened, refrigerate and consume within a few weeks.

Enjoying Your Preserves

Tomato preserves are a versatile addition to any pantry. Spread them on toast, use them as a glaze for meats, or stir into sauces for a burst of garden-fresh flavor. Each jar is a reminder of the summer garden, a testament to the joy and satisfaction of preserving the harvest.

Creating tomato preserves from your garden's bounty is a rewarding process that extends the pleasures of gardening into the colder months. It's a celebration of flavor, a nod to tradition, and a step towards sustainable living. With each batch, you not only preserve the taste of summer but also the memories of the gardening season that brought it to fruition.

HERBAL INFUSIONS AND BENEFITS

Within the verdant bounds of the garden, herbs flourish, offering more than their vibrant flavors—they are wellsprings of health and wellness, waiting to be tapped through the simple, ancient art of infusion. Herbal infusions harness the essence of these plants, extracting their potent benefits into water, the most elemental of solvents. This sub-chapter explores the alchemy of creating herbal infusions and delves into the myriad benefits they bring, from soothing the spirit to fortifying the body.

The Art of Herbal Infusions

At its core, an herbal infusion is the process of steeping herbs in hot water, allowing their flavors, aromas, and medicinal properties to meld with the liquid. This method, accessible and straightforward, requires no special equipment—just fresh or dried herbs and boiling water.

Making a Basic Herbal Infusion

- **Ingredients**: Fresh or dried herbs of your choice.
- **Procedure**:
    1. Boil water and remove it from heat.
    2. Add herbs to a teapot or jar. Use about one tablespoon of dried herbs or two tablespoons of fresh herbs per cup of water.
    3. Pour the hot water over the herbs, covering them completely.
    4. Steep for 5 to 15 minutes, depending on the desired strength.
    5. Strain the infusion into a cup, inhaling the aroma before taking the first sip.

Selecting Herbs for Infusion

- **Chamomile**: Renowned for its calming effects, chamomile is ideal for evening infusions to promote restful sleep.
- **Mint**:

Refreshing and invigorating, mint aids digestion and revitalizes the senses.

Lavender:

With its soothing fragrance, lavender is a balm for stress and anxiety. **Rosemary**: Known for enhancing memory and concentration, rosemary invigorates both mind and body.

- **Lemon Balm**: This herb lifts the spirit, easing stress and anxiety with its bright, citrusy notes.

Benefits of Herbal Infusions

- **Stress Reduction**: Herbs like lavender and chamomile are natural relaxants, helping to soothe the nerves and reduce stress.
- **Digestive Health**: Mint and ginger support digestion, relieving discomfort and promoting gut health.
- **Immune Support**: Echinacea and elderberry are champions of the immune system, bolstering the body's defenses.
- **Cognitive Benefits**: Rosemary and ginkgo biloba enhance cognitive function, improving memory and focus.
- **Antioxidant Properties**: Many herbs are rich in antioxidants, fighting oxidative stress and inflammation.

Tips for Perfecting Your Infusions

1. **Start with Fresh, High-Quality Herbs**: The potency and flavor of your infusion depend greatly on the quality of the herbs used. Whenever possible, use fresh herbs from your garden or source high-quality, organic dried herbs.
2. **Experiment with Blends**: Don't hesitate to combine herbs to create personalized blends. Consider both the health benefits and flavor profiles when crafting your mix.
3. **Mind the Temperature**: While boiling water is suitable for most herbs, some, like green tea leaves, prefer slightly cooler temperatures. Researching each herb's ideal steeping conditions can enhance the benefits and enjoyment of your infusion.

Nutritional Values

While specific nutritional values vary widely depending on the herbs used, most herbal infusions are low in calories yet rich in phytonutrients and antioxidants. They are hydrating, devoid of caffeine (with some exceptions, like green tea), and can be a calorie-free alternative to sugary beverages.

Herbal infusions stand at the intersection of simplicity and profundity, a testament to the garden's quiet power to nurture and heal. As we sip these brews, we partake in an age-old tradition of wellness, drawing closer to the natural world and its rhythms.

In crafting these infusions, we honor the herbs' myriad gifts—flavor, fragrance, and healing—bringing the essence of the garden into our daily lives, one cup at a time.

Herbs and infusions

Diving into the aromatic world of herbs, we discover each possesses unique properties that can be harnessed through the simple act of making infusions. Below is a curated list of 20 aromatic herbs, highlighting their distinct properties and the basic procedures for preparing their infusions to capture their essence and benefits.

1. Basil

- **Properties**: Anti-inflammatory, digestive aid
- **Infusion**: Steep 2 Tbsp fresh basil leaves in 1 cup boiling water for 8 min.

2. Peppermint

- **Properties**: Digestive health, mental clarity
- **Infusion**: Infuse 1 Tbsp dried peppermint leaves in 1 cup boiling water for 10 min.

3. Lemon Balm

- **Properties**: Stress relief, insomnia remedy
- **Infusion**: Use 1 Tbsp fresh lemon balm leaves per cup of boiling water, steep for 5 min.

4. Lavender

- **Properties**: Anxiety and stress relief, anti-inflammatory
- **Infusion**: Steep 1 tsp dried lavender flowers in 1 cup boiling water for 7 min.

5. Chamomile

- **Properties**: Sleep aid, digestive relaxant
- **Infusion**: Infuse 2 tsp dried chamomile flowers in 1 cup boiling water for 5 min.

6. Rosemary

- **Properties**: Cognitive function, hair growth
- **Infusion**: Steep 1 Tbsp fresh rosemary leaves in 1 cup boiling water for 10 min.

7. Thyme

- **Properties**: Antimicrobial, cough remedy
- **Infusion**: Use 2 tsp fresh thyme leaves per cup of boiling water, steep for 5 min.

8. Sage

- **Properties**: Antioxidant, memory enhancement
- **Infusion**: Infuse 1 Tbsp fresh sage leaves in 1 cup boiling water for 7 min.

9. Oregano

- **Properties**: Antioxidant, antibacterial
- **Infusion**: Steep 1 Tbsp fresh oregano leaves in 1 cup boiling water for 10 min.

10. Fennel

- **Properties**: Digestive aid, anti-inflammatory
- **Infusion**: Use 2 tsp crushed fennel seeds per cup of boiling water, steep for 10 min.

11. Dandelion

- **Properties**: Liver support, diuretic
- **Infusion**: Infuse 2 Tbsp fresh dandelion leaves in 1 cup boiling water for 10 min.

12. Nettle

- **Properties**: Iron source, allergy relief
- **Infusion**: Steep 1 Tbsp dried nettle leaves in 1 cup boiling water for 10 min.

13. Cilantro

- **Properties**: Heavy metal detoxification, digestive aid

- **Infusion**: Use 2 Tbsp fresh cilantro leaves per cup of boiling water, steep for 5 min.

14. Parsley

- **Properties**: Kidney health, rich in vitamins
- **Infusion**: Infuse 2 Tbsp fresh parsley leaves in 1 cup boiling water for 7 min.

15. Echinacea

- **Properties**: Immune system booster, cold and flu prevention
- **Infusion**: Steep 2 tsp dried echinacea flowers in 1 cup boiling water for 15 min.

16. Lemon Verbena

- **Properties**: Stress relief, digestive aid
- **Infusion**: Use 1 Tbsp fresh lemon verbena leaves per cup of boiling water, steep for 5 min.

17. Mint

- **Properties**: Digestive aid, nausea relief
- **Infusion**: Infuse 2 Tbsp fresh mint leaves in 1 cup boiling water for 7 min.

18. Ginger

- **Properties**: Nausea relief, anti-inflammatory
- **Infusion**: Steep 1 Tbsp fresh grated ginger in 1 cup boiling water for 10 min.

19. Marjoram

- **Properties**: Digestive aid, anti-inflammatory
- **Infusion**: Use 1 Tbsp fresh marjoram leaves per cup of boiling water, steep for 8 min.

20. Tarragon

- **Properties**: Appetite stimulant, sleep aid
- **Infusion**: Infuse 1 Tbsp fresh tarragon leaves in 1 cup boiling water for 5 min.

21. Catnip

- **Properties**: Stress relief, sleep aid
- **Infusion**: Steep 2 tsp dried catnip leaves in 1 cup boiling water for 10 min.

22. Calendula

- **Properties**: Skin health, anti-inflammatory

- **Infusion**: Infuse 1 Tbsp dried calendula flowers in 1 cup boiling water for 10 min.

23. Borage

- **Properties**: Adrenal support, mood lifter
- **Infusion**: Steep 1 Tbsp fresh borage leaves in 1 cup boiling water for 5 min.

24. Ashwagandha

- **Properties**: Stress reduction, vitality enhancer
- **Infusion**: Use 1 tsp dried ashwagandha root per cup of boiling water, steep for 15 min.

25. Valerian

- **Properties**: Sleep aid, anxiety relief
- **Infusion**: Infuse 1 tsp dried valerian root in 1 cup boiling water for 10 min.

26. Holy Basil (Tulsi)

- **Properties**: Stress relief, immune booster
- **Infusion**: Steep 2 Tbsp fresh holy basil leaves in 1 cup boiling water for 5 min.

27. Horehound

- **Properties**: Respiratory health, cough remedy
- **Infusion**: Use 2 tsp dried horehound leaves per cup of boiling water, steep for 10 min.

28. Hyssop

- **Properties**: Digestive aid, respiratory health
- **Infusion**: Infuse 1 Tbsp fresh hyssop leaves in 1 cup boiling water for 10 min.

29. Elderflower

- **Properties**: Immune support, cold and flu remedy
- **Infusion**: Steep 2 Tbsp dried elderflowers in 1 cup boiling water for 15 min.

30. Yarrow

- **Properties**: Fever reducer, digestive aid
- **Infusion**: Use 1 Tbsp dried yarrow flowers per cup of boiling water, steep for 10 min.

31. Spearmint

- **Properties**: Digestive aid, hormone balance
- **Infusion**: Infuse 2 Tbsp fresh spearmint leaves in 1 cup boiling water for 7 min.

32. Plantain Leaf

- **Properties**: Skin healing, anti-inflammatory
- **Infusion**: Steep 2 tsp fresh plantain leaves in 1 cup boiling water for 10 min.

33. Meadowsweet

- **Properties**: Pain relief, digestive health
- **Infusion**: Use 1 Tbsp dried meadowsweet flowers per cup of boiling water, steep for 10 min.

34. St. John's Wort

- **Properties**: Mood booster, nerve tonic
- **Infusion**: Infuse 1 Tbsp dried St. John's Wort in 1 cup boiling water for 10 min.

35. Feverfew

- **Properties**: Migraine relief, anti-inflammatory
- **Infusion**: Steep 1 tsp dried feverfew leaves in 1 cup boiling water for 10 min.

36. Lemon Grass

- **Properties**: Digestive health, calming

- **Infusion**: Use 2 Tbsp fresh lemongrass per cup of boiling water, steep for 10 min.

37. Burdock Root

- **Properties**: Blood purifier, skin health
- **Infusion**: Infuse 1 tsp dried burdock root in 1 cup boiling water for 20 min.

38. Goldenseal

- **Properties**: Immune support, digestive aid
- **Infusion**: Steep 1 tsp dried goldenseal root in 1 cup boiling water for 15 min.

39. Milk Thistle

- **Properties**: Liver support, detoxification
- **Infusion**: Use 1 tsp dried milk thistle seeds per cup of boiling water, steep for 15 min.

40. Anise Seed

- **Properties**: Digestive aid, cough suppressant
- **Infusion**: Infuse 1 Tbsp anise seeds in 1 cup boiling water for 15 min.

This expanded collection of herbs, from the calming effects of catnip to the digestive benefits of anise seed, underscores the profound versatility and power of plants. Preparing infusions from these herbs offers a simple yet profound way to integrate their healing and aromatic qualities into daily life. Whether seeking to calm the mind, uplift the spirit, or support physical health, these herbal infusions provide a natural, accessible means of nurturing well-being.

Remember, when exploring the use of herbs, especially for medicinal purposes, it's essential to consider individual health conditions and consult a healthcare professional as needed. The journey through the world of herbal infusions is a journey of discovery, connecting us more deeply to the wisdom of the natural world and the bounty of the garden.

Insights

Herb Infusions and Benefits: A Journey Through Time

The practice of making herb infusions is as ancient as civilization itself, with roots entwined in the very fabric of human history. These aromatic brews, steeped in tradition and lore, have been revered not only for their medicinal properties but also for their spiritual significance across cultures and continents.

Origins of Herb Infusions

The use of herb infusions originated in various parts of the world, with each culture discovering and developing its unique practices independently. The ancient Egyptians, renowned for their advances in medicine and herbalism, documented their use of herb infusions in Ebers Papyrus, one of the oldest medical texts known, dating back to around 1550 BCE. This text includes recipes for herb infusions meant to treat ailments ranging from fever to indigestion.

In China, the tradition of tea drinking, which began as an infusion of various herbs before the widespread use of Camellia sinensis (tea plant), has been a part of the culture since at least the Shang dynasty (1600–1046 BCE). The Chinese have long believed in the healing power of herbal teas, using them to promote health and longevity.

Similarly, in India, the practice of Ayurveda, an ancient system of medicine, has utilized herb infusions for thousands of years. Ayurvedic teas often include a complex blend of herbs designed to balance the body's three doshas (vital energies): Vata, Pitta, and Kapha.

Cultural Significance and Spread

The use of herbal infusions spread throughout the ancient world, from Greece and Rome to the Americas, with each civilization adding its own knowledge to the collective understanding of herbal medicine. The Greeks and Romans, for instance, were adept at using herbs for both culinary and medicinal purposes, with scholars like Hippocrates and Galen contributing significantly to the knowledge of medicinal plants. In the medieval period, monasteries played a crucial role in preserving and advancing the knowledge of herb infusions. Monks and nuns cultivated herb gardens, studying and documenting the properties of plants, and providing care for the sick. The monastery of St. Gall in Switzerland is famous for its detailed plan of a medieval garden that included specific areas for medicinal plants.

Medicinal Benefits

The renaissance of herbal medicine in recent times has brought a renewed interest in the health benefits of herb infusions. Modern research often supports ancient claims, highlighting the therapeutic potential of various herbs:

- **Chamomile**: Known for its calming properties, chamomile tea is used to reduce stress and improve sleep quality. It also has anti-inflammatory and antibacterial effects.

- **Peppermint**: Peppermint tea is praised for its ability to relieve digestive issues, such as bloating and indigestion. It also has a refreshing effect, helping to clear the mind.

- **Ginger**: Ginger tea is a powerful remedy for nausea and is often used to alleviate morning sickness in pregnant women. It also has anti-inflammatory properties, making it useful for pain relief.

- **Green Tea (Camellia sinensis)**: Rich in antioxidants, green tea is associated with numerous health benefits, including improved heart health, weight loss, and a lower risk of certain types of cancer.

Spiritual and Ritual Uses

Beyond their medicinal uses, herb infusions have also held spiritual significance. Many cultures have used herbal teas in rituals and ceremonies, believing in their power to cleanse, protect, and connect with the spiritual realm. For example, the Native Americans used sage and cedar infusions for purification and healing ceremonies, while in South America, yerba mate has been a centerpiece of social and ceremonial gatherings for centuries.

Modern Resurgence and Sustainability

Today, the popularity of herb infusions continues to grow, fueled by an increasing interest in natural and holistic approaches to health and wellness. This resurgence has also brought attention to the importance of sustainability in the cultivation and harvesting of medicinal herbs, with many consumers seeking out organic and ethically sourced products.

As we embrace the ancient wisdom of herb infusions, it's crucial to approach them with respect for their origins and an understanding of their role in the broader context of cultural practices and natural medicine. Whether used for health, relaxation, or spiritual awakening, herb infusions remain a testament to the enduring relationship between humans and the plant kingdom, a connection that nourishes body, mind, and soul.

In conclusion, the journey of herb infusions from ancient remedies to modern wellness practices is a rich tapestry that reflects the human quest for healing and harmony with nature. As we continue to explore and appreciate the vast world of herbal teas, we are not only tapping into ancient wisdom but also contributing to a legacy of health and healing that spans the ages.

CELEBRATING YOUR BOUNTY: HOSTING A GARDEN-TO-TABLE DINNER

Celebrating the bounty of your garden with a dinner shared among friends and family is one of the most gratifying experiences a gardener can have. It's a moment to showcase the fruits of your labor, a tangible feast made from the seeds you nurtured into a lush harvest. Hosting a garden-to-table dinner is not just about preparing a meal; it's about creating an atmosphere that reflects the beauty and abundance of the garden, connecting your guests directly to the source of their food, and celebrating the cycle of growth and nourishment.

EXAMPLE 1

Planning Your Garden-to-Table Dinner

Start by selecting a date when your garden is at its peak, offering a variety of fresh produce to highlight. Consider the flow of your space, whether you're setting a long table amidst the rows of your garden or bringing the garden's essence onto your patio or dining room. Ambient lighting, such as string lights or candles, can enhance the natural beauty of your setting.

Crafting the Menu

Your menu should be a reflection of what's currently flourishing in your garden. Begin with a walkthrough of your garden, noting which vegetables, fruits, and herbs are ripe and ready to be the stars of your dishes. Plan your menu around these ingredients, incorporating them into every course to truly celebrate their flavors.

- **Appetizers** might include fresh bruschetta topped with tomatoes and basil or zucchini fritters served with a yogurt-herb dip.
- **Main courses** can range from grilled vegetable platters drizzled with herb-infused oils to a savory tart filled with seasonal vegetables.
- **Desserts** could feature fruit crisps or tarts made from the berries or stone fruits of your garden, complemented by homemade herb ice cream.

Invitations

Send out invitations that hint at the garden theme, perhaps including a sprig of rosemary or a small packet of seeds. Encourage your guests to wear garden-appropriate attire and be prepared for an evening that delights the senses.

Table Setting

Decorate your table with elements from your garden. Use fresh flowers or herbs as centerpieces, and consider using leaves or pressed flowers as natural place cards. Serve dishes on platters that allow their colors and textures to shine, echoing the diversity of the garden.

The Dinner

Welcome your guests with a brief tour of your garden, sharing stories of the season's successes and challenges. This introduction sets the stage, making the meal an extension of the garden itself. As you serve each dish, describe its components and how they were grown, turning each bite into a deeper connection with the earth.

Engaging Your Guests

Encourage conversations about gardening, cooking, and the benefits of eating locally and seasonally. Share your experiences and tips, and invite guests to contribute their own. This exchange of knowledge enriches the meal and fosters a sense of community.

Tips for a Memorable Evening

1. **Prepare Ahead**: Choose dishes that can be made in advance or require minimal last-minute preparation to ensure you can enjoy the evening as much as your guests.

2. **Seasonal Beverages**: Offer drinks that complement the meal, such as herbal teas made from your garden or a signature cocktail featuring garden-fresh ingredients.

3. **Parting Gifts**: Send guests home with a small token from your garden, whether it's a jar of homemade preserves, a bundle of herbs, or a few fresh vegetables, extending the memory of the evening.

Hosting a garden-to-table dinner is a celebration of the garden's lifecycle, from seed to plate. It's an opportunity to share the beauty and abundance of the garden, creating a moment where time slows down, and the simple joys of food, friendship, and nature are savored. This gathering is a testament to the gardener's dedication and passion, an edible homage to the cycle of life that sustains us all. Through this communal experience, we're reminded of the deep connections we share with the earth, our food, and each other, fostering a sense of gratitude and wonder that lasts long after the last dish is cleared.

Certainly, let's expand on each topic within the context of hosting a garden-to-table dinner, offering additional ideas and insights to enrich the experience.

EXAMPLE 1

Planning Your Garden-to-Table Dinner

Expanding Idea: Incorporate a theme that complements the season or highlights a specific garden harvest, such as a "Midsummer Night's Feast" or "Autumn Harvest Celebration".

Planning around a theme can guide your menu choices, decorations, and even the dress code, creating a cohesive and immersive experience for your guests.

Crafting the Menu

Expanding Idea: Introduce a "from root to leaf" concept, where you aim to use as much of each plant as possible, minimizing waste and showcasing creativity. This could involve creating a pesto from carrot tops or beet greens, for example. Highlighting this approach in your menu educates your guests on sustainability while offering them a unique culinary experience.

Invitations

Expanding Idea: Alongside traditional or digital invitations, consider creating a small, informative booklet or a webpage about the featured plants in your garden. This could include interesting facts, gardening tips, or recipes. This approach not only sets the tone for your dinner but also engages your guests' curiosity and excitement beforehand.

Table Setting

Expanding Idea: Use vegetable and herb plants in small pots as part of your table decor, which guests can then take home. This living centerpiece is not only beautiful but also a gift that keeps on giving. You could also incorporate gardening tools as part of the decor, such as using small trowels as serving utensils for a playful touch.

The Dinner

Expanding Idea: For an interactive dinner, consider setting up cooking stations where guests can participate in making part of their meal, guided by you or a chef friend. For instance, a station for assembling their own herb butter or vinaigrette. This hands-on activity adds a fun and educational layer to the dining experience.

Engaging Your Guests

Expanding Idea: Organize a pre-dinner workshop or a talk on a topic related to gardening, sustainability, or cooking with fresh produce. This could be an informal discussion led by you or a guest speaker. Such an activity can spark interesting conversations and deepen the guests' appreciation of the dinner to follow.

Tips for a Memorable Evening

1. **Sustainability Practices**: Emphasize zero-waste practices throughout the dinner. Show how you compost, reuse, or recycle, and share tips on how guests can implement similar practices at home.

2. **Personal Touches**: Share personal stories about your gardening journey, the challenges you've faced, and the victories you've celebrated. This personal connection can make the evening more memorable and inspiring.

3. **Flexibility**: Be prepared to adapt your plans based on the unpredictable nature of gardening. Have a backup plan for ingredients that may not be as abundant as anticipated, and view it as an opportunity to be creative and spontaneous.

A garden-to-table dinner is more than a meal; it's a holistic experience that celebrates the cycle of life in the garden, the joys of harvesting and cooking, and the deep connections formed over shared food. By expanding on each aspect of the dinner with thoughtful details, sustainability practices, and engaging activities, you create an unforgettable evening that resonates with the beauty and abundance of the natural world, fostering a community of mindful eaters and garden enthusiasts.

As we close the pages of this journey from garden to table, we're reminded of the profound connection between the earth beneath our feet and the food on our plates. This book has not just been a guide to cultivating, harvesting, and preparing the bounty of your garden but an invitation to embrace a lifestyle deeply rooted in the rhythms of nature. Through each chapter, from turning the soil in spring to gathering around a bountiful table, we've explored the tangible and intangible rewards that gardening bestows upon us.

Gardening is more than a hobby or a means to produce food; it's a path to wellness, community, and sustainability. It teaches us patience, nurtures creativity, and fosters a sense of stewardship for the natural world. The act of planting a seed, nurturing its growth, and celebrating its harvest is a powerful metaphor for life—a cycle of growth, resilience, and renewal that mirrors our own experiences.

The recipes and stories shared within these pages are a testament to the joy and fulfillment that comes from connecting with the earth. They serve as a reminder that the simplest ingredients, when grown with love and prepared with care, can transform into meals that nourish both body and soul. This book encourages us to slow down, to savor the flavors of each season, and to share the fruits of our labor with those we love.

As we move forward, let us carry with us the lessons learned from the garden. Let us

be mindful of the impact of our choices on the environment, championing sustainability and biodiversity. Let us continue to explore the flavors and possibilities of garden-to-table cooking, pushing boundaries and discovering new favorites. And above all, let us never forget the magic that happens when we gather around a table, breaking bread and sharing stories, united by the food we've grown and the community we've built.

In the end, this book is more than a collection of gardening tips and recipes; it's an invitation to cultivate a life filled with growth, nourishment, and joy. May your garden flourish, your table always be full, and your heart be content in the knowledge that you are part of a cycle of life that is endlessly renewing and endlessly beautiful.

Cultivating Growth: Stories from the Earth

In the world of gardening, every plant, every garden, tells a story. These stories are not just about the growth of plants but about the personal growth and well-being of the gardeners who nurture them. "The Gardener's Bible" seeks to celebrate these stories, offering readers a tapestry of experiences that illuminate the profound connection between tending the earth and nurturing the soul. Here, we share tales of triumph, resilience, and discovery from gardeners who found in their patch of earth a source of joy, healing, and connection.

A Sanctuary of Peace

Sarah's story begins in the aftermath of personal loss. Seeking solace in the wake of her partner's passing, she turned to a neglected corner of her backyard. What started as a project to fill her days became a journey of healing. Each seed she planted was a step toward recovery, each day spent in the garden a day less burdened by grief. As her garden flourished, so too did Sarah. She found peace in the rhythmic routines of gardening, a connection to life's enduring cycles of loss and renewal. Her garden became a sanctuary, a living testament to the power of nurturing growth, both botanical and emotional.

Harvesting Health

Mark, a retired veteran, battled with chronic pain and the isolating effects of a long-term illness. On the recommendation of a friend, he began gardening as a form of physical therapy and a way to combat loneliness. The physical activity of digging, planting, and weeding became a natural pain management technique, improving his mobility and endurance. More unexpectedly, the social interactions that came with joining a community garden provided Mark a renewed sense of purpose and belonging. His health journey, mirrored by the seasonal cycles of his garden, reminds us that growth often comes from the most challenging conditions.

A Family's Bond

The Lopez family embarked on a gardening project to reduce their grocery bills and teach their children about the origins of food. What they didn't anticipate was how their small vegetable plot would grow into a cherished family ritual. Working side by side, parents and children learned the value of hard work, patience, and the rewards of harvest. The garden became a classroom, imparting lessons on biology, environmental science, and nutrition. But, more importantly, it became a space for laughter, conversation, and the strengthening of family bonds. Their story highlights the garden as a unifier, bringing people together in pursuit of a common goal.

Revitalizing a community

When a vacant lot in a struggling neighborhood became a dumping ground, Jasmine saw potential where others saw blight. Rallying her neighbors, she spearheaded the transformation of the neglected space into a vibrant community garden. The project faced numerous challenges, from securing funding to teaching novices how to garden. Yet, with persistence and collaboration, the garden flourished, becoming a source of pride and produce for the community. This communal effort not only beautified the neighborhood but also sowed seeds of empowerment, showing how shared spaces can foster a sense of collective responsibility and achievement.

The Journey of a Master Gardener

Tom's journey from novice to master gardener is a testament to lifelong learning and passion. Initially overwhelmed by the complexities of soil pH, pest management, and crop rotation, Tom's dedication to education transformed his approach to gardening. Through courses, mentorship, and trial and error, he honed his skills, eventually volunteering to teach others. His story is a reminder that gardening is a journey of continuous discovery, where the more we learn, the more we realize the depth of what remains to be discovered. Tom's evolution from student to teacher embodies the transformative power of gardening knowledge, not only in cultivating plants but in nurturing communities.

These stories, woven into the fabric of "The Gardener's Bible," serve as beacons of inspiration, demonstrating the myriad ways gardening touches our lives. Beyond providing food, beauty, and biodiversity, gardens offer spaces for healing, learning, connecting, and transforming. They remind us that in the act of caring for the earth, we also care for ourselves and each other, cultivating well-being alongside our plants. As readers turn these pages, it is our hope that they find not only guidance for growing gardens but also seeds of inspiration to grow their own stories of triumph, resilience, and connection.

Online Resources and Apps for Gardening

Gardening Apps

- **My Garden**: This comprehensive app allows you to plan your garden layout, track plant growth, and receive reminders for planting and watering schedules. It's an excellent tool for keeping your garden organized and healthy.
- **Picture This**: Struggling to identify a plant or pest in your garden? Picture This lets you snap a photo and receive instant identification and care tips. It's like having a botanist in your pocket.
- **From Seed to Spoon**: This app makes vegetable gardening easier by providing planting schedules, care instructions, and harvest tips based on your location. It also offers advice on companion planting and natural pest control methods.

Gardening Blogs

- **The Old Farmer's Almanac Blog**: A trusted source for generations, their blog continues to offer a mix of gardening tips, weather forecasts, and folklore. It's perfect for gardeners who appreciate a blend of tradition and science.
- **Gardenia**: For those seeking design inspiration and practical advice, Gardenia offers beautifully curated content on garden design, DIY projects, and plant care.
- **Epic Gardening**: Kevin Espiritu shares his expertise through easy-to-follow guides, product reviews, and innovative gardening techniques. His focus on urban and hydroponic gardening is particularly valuable for those with limited space.

Gardening Forums

- **Garden Web**: Hosted by Houzz, this forum offers a platform for gardeners to share experiences, exchange advice, and provide support to one another. The diverse community ensures that you can find information on almost any gardening topic.

- **Reddit's r/gardening**: This subreddit is a treasure trove of gardening wisdom, personal projects, and a supportive community eager to help with any gardening challenge you might face.

- **The National Gardening Association's Garden.org**: Offers a comprehensive forum where novices and experts alike can discuss gardening techniques, plant identification, and much more. The community's knowledge base is vast and welcoming.

YouTube Channels

- **Garden Answer**: Laura LeBoutillier's passion for gardening shines through in her detailed tutorials, garden tours, and DIY landscaping projects. Her channel is both informative and inspiring for gardeners at any level.

- **Charles Dowding**: An advocate for no-dig gardening, Charles shares his expertise on creating productive vegetable gardens with minimal soil disturbance. His practical advice and calm demeanor make gardening feel accessible to everyone.

By integrating these online resources and apps into your gardening practice, you can expand your knowledge, solve problems more efficiently, and connect with a global community of gardening enthusiasts. "The Vegetable Gardener's Bible" encourages readers to leverage these digital tools to enhance their gardening experience, ensuring that the wisdom of the past blooms hand in hand with the innovations of the present.

Conclusion: Cultivating a Legacy with "The Vegetable Gardener's Bible"

As we turn the final page of "The Vegetable Gardener's Bible," we are not merely closing a book; we are opening the gate to a garden brimming with possibilities. Through this journey, we have delved deep into the soil of knowledge, planting seeds of wisdom that, when nurtured, promise to transform bare plots into bountiful gardens. This bible has been more than a guide; it has been a companion, whispering to us the age-old secrets of the earth, teaching us the rhythms of the seasons, and showing us the way to harmonize with the natural world.

The Heart of Gardening

At its heart, gardening is an act of love—an expression of our deepest connection to the cycle of life. It is a testament to the resilience of both the human spirit and the earth itself. In each chapter of this bible, from understanding the foundations of vegetable gardening to mastering the art of harvesting, storing, and preserving, we have been reminded of this profound bond. We have learned that to tend a garden is to tend to ourselves, nurturing our bodies, minds, and spirits in the process.

The Wisdom of the Earth

"The Vegetable Gardener's Bible" has taught us to listen—to truly listen—to the wisdom of the earth. It has shown us that the soil under our fingernails is not just dirt, but a living, breathing entity, teeming with life and eager to give. We have learned that water, that most precious resource, is to be cherished and conserved, that mulch is a guardian of moisture and life, and that the right balance of nutrients can turn a struggling plant into a thriving powerhouse.

The Community of Gardeners

This journey has also revealed the beauty of the gardening community—a tapestry of individuals united by a common love for the earth. Through the pages of this bible, we have joined a centuries-old fellowship of gardeners, each contributing their thread to the ever-evolving story of cultivation. We have shared in the trials and triumphs of gardeners past and present, learning from their experiences and adding our own discoveries to the collective wisdom.

The Future of Gardening

Looking forward, "The Vegetable Gardener's Bible" leaves us with a vision of the future—a future where gardens flourish in every space, from sprawling rural fields to compact urban balconies. It paints a picture of a world where sustainable practices and a deep respect for nature guide our hands, where the health of the soil is as important as the health of those it feeds. It is a future where the lessons contained in these pages are passed down through generations, ensuring that the art of gardening continues to grow and adapt.

A Personal Harvest

As individual gardeners, we each harvest something unique from this bible. For some, it may be the confidence to plant their first seedling; for others, a newfound commitment to organic practices. Perhaps it's a deeper understanding of the intricate dance between pests and plants, or the inspiration to preserve the summer's bounty through canning and fermenting. Whatever the harvest, it is rich with the promise of growth.

Cultivating a Legacy

In the end, "The Gardener's Bible" Vegetable is more than a collection of gardening techniques—it is a call to cultivate a legacy. It urges us to leave the earth richer than we found it, to nurture not just gardens but communities, to share the fruits of our labor with neighbors and friends, and to teach the next generation the value of a seed well planted.

As we step back into our gardens, let us carry the lessons of this bible with us. Let us be mindful stewards of the land, compassionate members of our communities, and generous sharers of the abundance we create. Let us garden with joy, with respect for the past, and with hope for the future.

In closing, "The Vegetable Gardener's Bible" is not just a guide to growing vegetables; it is a manifesto for living—a life deeply rooted in the rhythms of nature, enriched by the act of gardening, and blossoming with the potential for abundance and joy. As we continue our gardening journeys, let this bible be our guide, our inspiration, and our reminder of the beauty and bounty that await in the humble act of planting a seed.

In embracing both the timeless teachings of "The Vegetable Gardener's Bible" and the dynamic resources available through modern technology, we weave a rich tapestry of knowledge and community. This harmonious blend of ancient wisdom and contemporary innovation offers a powerful example for new generations. It demonstrates that while the tools and techniques of gardening may evolve, the

essence of nurturing the earth remains constant. As we pass this knowledge on, we do more than teach the next generation how to tend a garden; we instill in them a respect for nature, a commitment to sustainability, and the joy of growing. This legacy, enriched by the wisdom of the past and the possibilities of the future, is a precious gift—one that holds the seeds of hope, resilience, and connection for generations to come.

In the verdant tapestry of life, gardens hold a special place—sanctuaries where nature's rhythms are not just observed but deeply felt. Within the pages of "The Vegetable Gardener's Bible," we've journeyed through the intricacies of cultivating the earth, a voyage that transcends the mere act of planting seeds and tending to plants. It is a profound dialogue with nature, a testament to the resilience and bounty of the earth. This book serves not only as a guide to the practical aspects of gardening but also as a repository of wisdom, a compendium of the soul-enriching relationship between humans and the soil.

The true beauty of this bible lies in its potential to be a beacon for future generations, a legacy of knowledge and passion for the earth that we are called to pass down. Gardening, in its essence, is an act of hope—a belief in the morrow, an investment in the future. As such, "The Vegetable Gardener's Bible" emerges not just as a manual for the present generation of gardeners but as a priceless heirloom for those yet to come.

In an age where digital screens often disconnect us from the natural world, teaching our children the art and science of gardening becomes an act of reconnection. It's a way to ground them in the physical world, to instill a sense of responsibility for the environment, and to awaken awe for the cycle of life. This book, with its wealth of knowledge and insight, becomes a crucial tool in this endeavor. It offers lessons that extend beyond gardening to encompass values of sustainability, patience, and stewardship.

By engaging with the younger generation through gardening, we offer them more than just the skills to grow food. We provide them with a framework for understanding the interconnectedness of life, the importance of caring for our planet, and the joy of nurturing growth. "The Vegetable Gardener's Bible" stands as a testament to these lessons, a guide that illuminates the path to a more sustainable and mindful way of living.

Furthermore, this bible emphasizes the community aspect of gardening—the shared experiences, the collective wisdom, and the communal joys of harvest. In teaching the next generation to garden, we're inviting them into a global community that transcends borders and cultures, united by a common love for the earth. It's a lesson in collaboration and respect, showing that together, we can create abundance and beauty in even the smallest of spaces.

As we conclude, it's clear that "The Vegetable Gardener's Bible" is more than just a book; it's a beacon for the future, a compilation of knowledge and wisdom that we are entrusted to pass on to the new gardeners of the world. It calls upon us to sow the seeds of understanding and respect for nature in young hearts and minds, cultivating a generation that values the earth and its gifts.

In sharing this bible with the new generation, we do more than teach them to garden; we inspire them to become caretakers of the planet, advocates for sustainability, and champions of the natural world. We equip them with the tools to forge a greener, more bountiful future, ensuring that the legacy of "The Vegetable Gardener's Bible" flourishes in gardens and hearts for generations to come.

Thus, as we turn the final page, let us commit to this noble task of transmission, ensuring that the wisdom contained within these pages continues to inspire, guide, and enrich the lives of gardeners young and old. In doing so, we honor the past, cherish the present, and seed a hopeful, verdant future.

While I can't generate a response exactly 1000 words long, I can certainly craft a thoughtful conclusion that acknowledges the readers' choice and highlights the importance of passing on the wisdom contained in "The Vegetable Gardener's Bible" to future generations. Here's a concise version:

In closing, "The Vegetable Gardener's Bible" extends beyond the pages of advice, tips, and techniques; it embodies a legacy of knowledge, a connection to the earth, and a testament to the transformative power of gardening. This book is not just a compilation of gardening wisdom—it's a living, evolving story that each of you contributes to with every seed you plant, every garden you nurture, and every harvest you celebrate.

As we reach the end of our journey together, it's essential to recognize that the true essence of this book is not just in cultivating gardens but in cultivating lives enriched with patience, care, and a profound connection to the natural world. The principles, practices, and philosophies shared within these pages stand as a testament to the timeless bond between humans and the earth—a bond that, when nurtured, yields not only bountiful harvests but also a bountiful spirit.

To all who have chosen to embark on this journey through "The Vegetable Gardener's Bible," thank you. Your choice reflects a desire not only to grow gardens but to grow as individuals and communities, deeply rooted in the rhythms of nature and the cycles of life. It is a choice that honors the past, enriches the present, and seeds the future. Let this book be a beacon for the new generations, guiding them through the challenges and joys of gardening. May they find within its pages the inspiration to explore, the knowledge to thrive, and the wisdom to sustain. And as they turn the soil, plant the seeds, and nurture their gardens, may they also nurture a world that values sustainability, community, and the sheer joy of watching something grow.

In gratitude, we thank you for choosing "The Vegetable Gardener's Bible." May your gardens—and your lives—flourish abundantly. Here's to the generations of gardeners to come, may they inherit a world as beautiful and bountiful as the gardens we've tended together.

Made in United States
Orlando, FL
15 June 2024

47893176R00111